A NEW PARADIGM FOR

UNDERSTANDING YOUTH CULTURE

BLUR

JEFF KEUSS

PRAISE FOR *BLUR*

Think of *Blur* as a conversation about ministering to youth with one of the most intelligent, experienced, and compassionate people you know. Don't expect programmed, easy answers. Keuss offers a view of ministry that helps teens move toward the "very heartbreaking reality of who we are—we're called to a life of direction, release, and ultimate integration with our Creator—a poetic integration that's prepared in advance for us to do." This includes meeting teens at the wells in their lives, walking beside them on their journeys, and offering glimpses of a life that looks more like a narrative quest than a how-to book. This book challenged my assumptions, fired my imagination, and confirmed the power of "the life poetic."

> Maureen McQuerry, author of
> *The Peculiars* and *Beyond the Door*

Wow! *Blur* is a thoughtful, practical, and compassionate exploration of youth culture and faith from a theologian who has thought deeply about both. Packed with rich insights, this is a must read for anyone trying to faithfully understand and love the younger generation.

> Dick Staub, author of *The Culturally-Savvy Christian*
> and founder of *The Kindlings Muse* podcast

I deeply appreciate the work that Jeff Keuss has done, both as a father of two teens and as a youth worker for the last twenty-five years. While there is much to be said about the impact of culture and new media on today's young people, *Blur* reminds us that relationships centered on the incarnational, redemptive, and missional power of God's story can still change young people's lives.

> Brian Muchmore, executive director, Youth for Christ

Conversant in the most recent trends in youth ministry, plus everything from Bonhoeffer to Björk, Jeff Keuss has greatly added to the canon of scholarship in youth ministry with *Blur*. Keuss's concept of "sacredly mobile youth" puts a name on what many of us have been observing in recent years. This book is destined to be a conversation piece in youth ministry studies for years to come.

Tony Jones, distinguished lecturer in the practice
of theology at United Theological Seminary
of the Twin Cities and author of
Postmodern Youth Ministry

A NEW PARADIGM FOR

UNDERSTANDING YOUTH CULTURE

BLUR

JEFF KEUSS

ZONDERVAN

Blur
Copyright © 2014 by Jeff F. Keuss

YS Youth Specialties is a trademark of YOUTHWORKS!, INCORPORATED and is registered with the United States Patent and Trademark Office.

This title is also available as a Zondervan ebook.
Visit www.zondervan.com/ebooks.

Requests for information should be addressed to:
Zondervan, *Grand Rapids, Michigan 49530*

Library of Congress Cataloging-in-Publication Data

Keuss, Jeffrey F., 1965-
     Blur : a new paradigm for understanding youth culture / Jeff Keuss.
        pages cm
     Includes bibliographical references.
     ISBN 978-0-310-51484-8 (softcover) — ISBN 978-0-310-51485-5 (ebook)
     1. Church work with youth. 2. Youth. I. Title.
   BV4447.K48 2013
   259'.23—dc23

Cover design: LUCAS Art & Design
Cover photography: Masterfile
Interior design: David Conn

Printed in the United States of America

13 14 15 16 17 18 19 /DCI/ 20 19 18 17 16 15 14 13 12 11 10 9 8 7 6 5 4 3 2 1

CONTENTS

A TALE OF TWO WILLIAMS

I'm a theologian who is deeply concerned about young people. In my work as a youth director and pastor of churches both in the United States and the United Kingdom over the past twenty years, I've been blessed to have many encounters with youth. Throughout these pages I'll reference some studies on youth faith development as well as some of my own experiences. It is my hope that this book will help you better understand the young people you've either encountered or will encounter in the future.

Let me begin by introducing you to two young men I've had the opportunity to serve: I'll call them "William 1.0" and "William 2.0." They represent much of the promise I hope you'll see as you open your eyes to the many ways God is working and moving in today's young people.

Recently, I was having coffee with a young man in my church, William 2.0, and our time together evoked one of these sanctified *déjà vu* moments, if you will. The moment reverberated with so many encounters of people around "watering holes": those places where we find people seeking to quench their thirst and find companionship. Meetings at watering holes are big in Scripture. We see this in the accounts of Abraham's servant finding Rebekah, the future wife of Isaac, at the well of Nahor (Gen. 24:10-61); Jacob meeting Rachel at the well in Harran (Gen. 29:1-20); and Moses receiving Zipporah as his wife after he rescued the seven daughters of Reuel at the well in Midian (Ex. 2:16-22).

"Wells" in youth ministry can be many things: events that open up young people to hearing the gospel in new and transformative ways; a particular book, movie, or song that grabs a teenager's attention and leads him to ask deeper and more sustaining questions that will propel him into the arms of Christ; and relationships forged with mentors and communities that help youth see their identities in the Holy Spirit who has been working on their behalf before they were even born.

To locate the well of a young person is to find that it's a combination of things not easily discerned—things that seem to draw together at particular moments. Picture tide pools on the shoreline that are separate and distinct at low tide, but at full tide they become a large pool in which one can swim betwixt and between, making the connection in movement and purpose. Like the wells of the Bible where people meet and find new meaning, the wells of young people aren't merely places, people, or cultural products such as a books or songs. Instead, they can be one thing and a collection of things all at the same time, depending on what's occurring in the journey of the young person's faith. This well where I met William 2.0 represents such a time. His was a deep well, one that went far below the surface and—as with quite a bit of youth ministry—required work to draw out what was in there.

I met with William 2.0 as part of a confirmation class requirement that all young people in our church must complete if they wish to become members of the church. Many of our youth look forward to this class as an opportunity to dig deeper into Christian tradition, read Christian Scripture, and be mentored by an adult in the congregation. I was partnered with William 2.0 with the intention that we would meet regularly, build a theological friendship of sorts, and pray together throughout the six-month class.

At this particular meeting, we sat across from each other with our respective drinks in hand, and he continually prodded his cell phone as it lay on the table, as if to check its pulse. I began the conversation with the seemingly benign question, "So . . . how are things with your soul?"

William 2.0 is an introverted young man who has grown up in the church. His family loves him dearly, supports his extracurricular interests, and gives him autonomy while also providing good boundaries. When I asked about friends, he didn't have many to speak of other than classmates he saw only at school. As an honors student, he's never struggled with school, yet he's indifferent to it. He's interested in comic books and video games—not obsessively, but they're important to him. William 2.0's world includes the church but is in no way bounded by it. He's a reader of sci-fi novels and has watched all of the Star Wars films. (We both dislike the later additions to the series, and our distain for the character Jar Jar Binks was a moment of connection, to be sure.) These fictional universes have given him the metanarrative for his life: honor, courage, adventure, and the quest for something more.

But over and over again as I asked about specific issues pertaining to the Christian faith and Scripture, he would look at me, pause, and say, "I'm fine." Drawing water from deep wells takes work.

In John's gospel, Jesus encounters the Samaritan woman in the middle of his "Cana to Cana" travels between John 2:1-12 at the wedding of Cana (Jesus' Jewish disciples come to believe he's the Christ through his miracle of turning water into wine), and John 4:43-54 where Jesus heals the son of a royal official in Cana (this official from a non-Jewish household comes to believe in Jesus through Jesus' word). Overall, the placement of the account of Jesus' conversation with the Samaritan woman encourages us to watch this encounter and see it as central between the bookend visits to Cana: the first with a Jewish audience, and the second with a non-Jewish audience.

Meetings at deep wells blur our categories and put us betwixt and between destination points. We're neither "here" nor "there," but we're certainly in a place where we can pause along the way—a moment in the midst of motion. These meetings at wells help us see that encounters with the divine don't nail us to the ground, nor does God stand before us fixed like a statue. Much like the swirling dance of the Trinity that moves and embraces us in the perpetual love of the Father, Son, and Holy Spirit, so, too, do the moving waters of the deep well swell to meet us in a motion that's often blurred and hard to discern. Ultimately we must be led by faith. This is important to recall as we discuss what it means to work with youth as "sacredly mobile adolescents," a phrase I'll return to in other sections of the book.

What we see in the heart of God's identity as the Trinity is a constant and perpetual movement that's far from static. If we're to take seriously the words of Genesis 1:26-27 that say we've been created in the image of God and that this image of God is the fullness of the Trinity, this has huge implications for how we see and experience each other and the young people in our ministries. The Father, Son, and Holy Spirit are distinct persons, yet they're known most completely in the community they have with one another in a perpetual act of giving and receiving love. In this way the young people God has given us to nurture and learn from in faith are first and foremost *sacred* in that they're created in the image and likeness of God.

Therefore, that identity supplants any other cultural identity that they—or we—may impose upon them.

Second, they're *mobile* in that the deepening and forging of their identities is best understood as a constant process of movement and growth through building relationships, acquiring new spiritual disciplines that will grow and change over time, and resourcing their faith from an ever-changing culture that will require change as they grow.

Finally, young people are in a particular point of development—they're *adolescents*, after all—and we must not attempt to force them to speed through this time too quickly. We must also be cautious not to overly romanticize or delimit youth in extreme ways where we view them from a perspective of either pure innocence or absolute debauchery. As adolescents they're fully embodied human beings, not merely thinking, rational entities devoid of emotions or physical bodily expression.

As will be discussed in later sections of the book, some social theorists continue to categorize teens in ways that overly emphasize reason at the expense of living, breathing, moving life that doesn't always fit into easily defined categories. As I reflect on William 2.0, it isn't his ability to answer questions that matters; what's important is who he is in body, soul, spirit . . . as well as mind.

In this way my meeting with William 2.0 had the resonance of biblical accounts of people who met at deep wells: there was expectation, intention, a blending of family connections and relationships we shared, and—on the surface of things—a level of mundane immanence that merged past events with future expectations resourced by multiple faith traditions and high, low, and popular culture. William 2.0 and I were on a journey, and both of us were trying to find something in our connection with each other that neither of us could fully articulate. Like Jesus and the woman at the well's rather plain exchange regarding drinking water, my verbal probing of William 2.0 as to the state of his soul was met with, "Yes," "No," and "Fine," and the conversation seemed to move forward only with a discussion of school and what he was having for lunch.

In 1987, I sat across from William 1.0 in a McDonald's, and we had a conversation about a confirmation class he was taking. This was during an era before cell phones and other handheld devices, and William 1.0 occupied himself in a more carnal way: ketchup packets that he'd stacked like a pile of tomato-embossed Lincoln Logs. As I earnestly probed William 1.0 about the state of his soul, he also offered answers such as "Yes," "No," and "Fine," while intermittently squeezing ketchup into his mouth in a slow yet ordered succession, systematically whittling down the packets into a pile of empty condiment sleeping bags.

William 1.0 loved to play Dungeons & Dragons. He was in a gifted math program at his school. And for the two years that he was involved in the youth program, he rarely wore anything other than a Washington Huskies sweatshirt, old jeans, and black Converse tennis shoes. He never combed his mop of tangled hair, and he had a strong foot odor that became so overpowering in the church van during a mission trip that I felt obliged to have a hygiene conversation with him on a curb in rural West Virginia.

William 1.0 and 2.0 don't know each other, their youth is separated by twenty-five years, they came from distinct families, they went to different schools, they were influenced by different seasons of national and global politics and economics, they had different cultural heroes, and they have different developmental narratives in relation to technology. Yet much like the Scripture narratives of meetings that occurred at wells—meetings that spanned hundreds of years, as well as different cultures and ethnicities—my encounters with William

1.0 and 2.0 broke through the space-time continuum through a theological wormhole and reflected each other in profound ways.

My meeting with William 1.0 in that 1980s McDonald's ended without any observable spiritual transformation. When we got up from the table and he collected the empty ketchup packets, there were no lasting catch phrases in my mind for that evening. There were no Scripture passages upon which to place an Ebenezer we could show the coming generations to prove that something of God had appeared in this place, at this time, to these people. Like thousands of other McDonald's restaurants that have stood as voiceless sentinels on the global landscape, where people find solace in fast food rather than deep conversation, this one offered no way to mark our time and conversation. As far as I could tell, the hour and a half had been a minor failure. William 1.0 was still seemingly indifferent to the power of God in his life and seemed content to remain in the youth group as a fringe character who liked painting D&D figures in his garage after school and ate his ketchup straight, no chaser.

As the years passed, William 1.0 left the youth group and the church, and I also moved on and into other seasons of my life. I will freely admit that although I invested significant time with him, we departed from each other's lives in a way that was akin to T. S. Eliot's world ending in "The Hollow Men": "Not with a bang but a whimper." And when I stood up after my meeting with William 2.0 in the twenty-first century, I had many of the same feelings I'd had regarding my time with William 1.0—there was nothing I could point to that made this a holy exchange of any sort. A qualitative study of the transcript recording our exchange would show words such as *Yoda, Robopocalypse*, and *scouting* as the dominant terms—not words such as *saved, convicted, grace, cross, prayer, baptism,* or any of the thousands of other terms that church folks will notice as part of the tradition of faith. I felt like I was living out Bill Murray's role in *Groundhog Day* sans the Sonny and Cher track—I was stuck in a repetitious cycle, and I had no discernible ability to effect sustainable transformation.

Let me pause for a moment to reflect on this recounting of my time spent with William 1.0 and 2.0, as these encounters and others like them will underscore an important point for the thesis of *Blur*: This book is about the real, on-the-ground, day-to-day lives of young people who've been claimed, taken, broken open, and released in powerful, deep, and abiding ways by the work of the Holy Spirit. Yet we often encounter only momentary blips on the divine radar screen. Sometimes we find each other in movement toward readily discernible locations on the spectrum of the orthodox Christian faith, and other times—such as with my encounters with the Williams—leave me fearful that I haven't done enough or the church hasn't done enough to shore up and lock down within these youth a concrete commitment to the cross.

As I will share in the narratives that follow, it's the role of the church and those committed to the lives of young people to put away their panic and fear and become the gospel fully present both for and with them—whatever the outcome. To minister to youth in this culture will mean entering into a whirlwind-like blur of culture, faith traditions, personalities, hopes, disappointments, and love both ordered and disordered. To put a stronger point on it, the prime directive of ministering to youth isn't getting these individuals to Jesus—for Jesus is already with them if we would have eyes to see and ears to hear. Our prime directive is to love them as Jesus does and enter into the chaos-like blur of their lives. We're to sit with them like Job's friends did and await the fullness of God together, no matter the cost to our preconceived, overly programmed, ends-justify-the-means, bullet-pointed youth ministry strategies.

What I've learned in the twenty-five years since I first sat across from William 1.0 and earnestly watched him deconstruct condiment packets in silence is that much of what we do in youth ministry has to be held in trust for the long road. And we need to do less rather than more—especially in regard to programming. As I sat in my meeting with William 2.0, I began by trusting in the promise of the covenant that appears throughout the Bible: "I will be your God, and you will be my people." It's a call to profound patience and trust in the movement of God.

And this is why: Fast-forward from 1987 to 2005—I received an email from William 1.0. He'd wanted to track me down for a while and, thanks to the wonders of the Web, he'd found my email address and even some of my online sermons. He told me he was married with two children; he'd gone to university and then graduate school; and he was working at a local hospital. No, he wasn't active in a church—although he attends one every now and then—nor was he looking to join one. But after his children were born, he remembered youth group and just wanted to find me and say hello. From what I could tell, he's a good man, a caring soul, and a generous person to his family and workplace. He has a quiet way of speaking that was evident even as a teenager—there's not a lot of certainty in his pronouncements, but he has a calm peacefulness that's larger than loud declarations about the faith.

After this exchange I was reminded of Karl Barth's words in *Church Dogmatics* in that (referring to Jesus' life in God the Father):

> The God who reconciled the world and therefore the Christian to Himself, and who does not cease to reveal Himself as the One who did so, is for him in either case, on this way

which is both difficult and glorious. This is what makes the life of the Christian possible, necessary and meaningful in this time. This is what makes him in all circumstances a positive man. His life is positive in the fact that from the very first it is one long calling upon God. He calls upon God representatively for those who do not yet do so, or do not seem to do so. He does not exclude but includes them when he prays to this God: "Our Father! Hallowed be thy name! Thy kingdom come! Thy will be done on earth, as it is in heaven!" This God will not faint, neither be weary. He hears all those who call on Him in this way.[1]

In many respects after hearing from William 1.0 after all those years, I was convicted in that moment that these young people we work with in our programs are the embodiment of this "one long calling upon God." While we actively pursue and shape them through all we do, we know that ultimately they're in the embrace of God despite our best efforts. God is in the mix. God is pursuing each and every one of us. God is the Author of true and abiding love, and we know he's patient. God is kind. God is just. And we're not forsaken. Ever.

We know this, but do we exist in a repose of trust and patience where we can watch young people like William 1.0 and 2.0 move freely in and out of our programs, experience all that we can offer, and walk out our doors without making a statement of faith? At a recent gathering of youth program directors funded by the Lilly Foundation, I was asked to respond to the following questions: "What do you think the young people you serve would hope that people concerned about leadership in the church might learn from their stories? And where in our systems of Christian formation might we find other spaces that similarly transform young people who become Christian

---

1. Karl Barth, *Church Dogmatics IV.3.1: The Doctrine of Reconciliation*, 1st ed. (New York: T&T Clark International, 2004), 367.

leaders?" I immediately thought of the twinned stories of William 1.0 and 2.0 as I reflected on what my response would be to this group of dedicated leaders of important youth programs. After I prayed about it, I offered the following: "While I'm not assuming that salvation just happens without our working with the Holy Spirit in relationships with teens of the William 1.0 or 2.0 ilk, I'm convinced that the arc of history extends further than the season in which we'll have them in our respective programs."

The testimonies of many of the youth who have come through these programs—and thousands of church and parachurch ministries over the decades—show that deep and meaningful experiences have happened and will continue to happen. Youth are meeting the living Lord. Young people are turning to face Jesus and walk into the light of salvation with all their heart, soul, and strength. Leaders for the future of the church are gaining a vision of the gospel in junior and senior high ministries every day.

But I believe my exchanges with both William 1.0 and 2.0 also represent an encounter at deep wells that we'll never fully comprehend. We can't time-stamp the event horizon when the journey will rise to its apogee. William 1.0 reminded me that God is constantly calling through whispers, moans, exclamations, and twenty-five years of silence. The Catholic theologian Hans Urs von Balthasar reminds us that human beings are in one respect "like" God in their capacity to name and order the world, but in another respect human beings are limited—a part of nature—which means their capacity to name what's happening to them is also limited:

> [A person's] capacity for transcendence in itself is no guarantee that he will attain the end for which he was created. This must come to him in freedom. In himself, he constitutes the boundary that divides the world from God, and it is for

him to order the things in this world with a view to his own transcendence. He must therefore relate the world to that which lies beyond him, knowing of himself the goal toward which he ought to set his face. The shadows of contradiction lengthen as guilt and death steal over him. He is unable to shut himself up in his own finitude nor enclose himself in his own mortality (for these are realities of his life), leaving the future in the hands of an anonymous ongoing human race and a Providence that has no name, nor can he behave as if his death counted for nothing, and therefore simply busy himself with the usual interests men pursue, preoccupied as they are with the technical administration of the world of things, in which death seems to be of no ultimate significance. The mystery of their being never ceases to nag at him in every possible way.[2]

As you journey through the chapters of *Blur*, I hope young people like William 1.0 and 2.0 hold sway before you and challenge you not to be too quick to categorize or limit their capacity for change. I also hope we can learn to listen and relax into our calling to work within youth culture and the young people we'll meet in the whirlwind-like blur of this day and age. When I think of the young people I've had the chance to serve in ministry over the years and then watch grow to adulthood, I'm reminded over and over again of God's sustaining providence and care for those he loves.

When I asked William 1.0 what to share as I began writing this book, he said, "Perhaps tell them something like 'deeply trust in the Lord and let love pour out of you as you see me sitting there sucking down ketchup packets. It's not over when you think it is. Do your research, read your theology, believe in Scripture in ways that make it a living Word before my

---

2. Hans Urs von Balthasar, *Engagement with God: The Drama of Christian Discipleship* (San Francisco: Ignatius Press, 2006), 83.

generation. But please be patient. I don't know yet what's going on in my soul, but perhaps I will someday. Your job? Be faithful, relax, and love.'"

Wow.

That sums up much of what I hope you glean from the chapters that follow. Like Balthasar, I truly believe "the mystery of their very being never ceases to nag at them in every possible way," and perhaps that's enough.

When I said goodbye to William 2.0 last week, I didn't worry as I did twenty-five years ago. I just smiled and was thankful for his life. By the way, a few days later I got another email. William 2.0 asked me to speak to his Boy Scout troop about my job. Sure, it's not quite the same as praying the Sinner's Prayer with someone, but it's certainly better than watching a person eat ketchup straight up.

CHAPTER 1

BLURRING
DEFINITIONS

Learning to Meet Youth Where They Are

Prior to my work as a pastor and theologian, I worked as a district executive for the Boy Scouts of America. One of the largest youth social service organizations in the world, the Boy Scouts of America was founded in the United States in 1910 following the model of youth leadership formation put forward in Britain by Lord Robert Baden-Powell. Core to Baden-Powell's vision was the importance of providing focused adult mentorship and training for young people in order to instill character traits of honor, courage, and charity, regardless of social class. Baden-Powell was a committed Christian, and much of the growth in scouting during the last century has been through aligning many of the ideals found in the gospel with the organization of the Boy Scouts.

I served a large area of greater Seattle by training volunteer leaders and helping to form new dens, packs, and troops in community centers, schools, and churches. I also worked with groups of young people to help them connect and grow in these community-based scout groups. At an organizing event at an elementary school one evening, I was pulled aside by a mother and her young son. She told me her son had made friends in his troop, and she truly enjoyed seeing him grow in his self-confidence. "His patrol group even has a Bible study," she exclaimed. I told her that many scout groups had found that having faith be central to life together in community was an authentic way for a number of the scouting ideals to be lived out. "I can see that," she replied and then followed up with an interesting comment: "The youth pastor of the church where our Boy Scout troop meets spoke to the troop about the church's youth ministry and encouraged the boys to attend. The problem is, the scout meetings are on the same evening as the youth group. Our scoutmaster has asked the youth group to meet at a different time, and the response was to ask the troop to change their meeting time. It's been a standoff for quite a while." She then said, "If my son is growing in faith and maturity where he is, why should I take him away from that?"

This question of having to choose between meaningful, generative programs isn't unusual. Many parents battle the challenges of time commitments with sports, music lessons, and, of course, church and parachurch groups. But what do you say if a young person is growing in faith—yet not in an expressly Christian context? In this woman's case, she and her son attended regular Sunday worship services, but the peer faith community and adult mentorship in faith wasn't going to happen in a church or parachurch—instead, it was happening in the Boy Scout context. Was she making a poor choice for her son? What was evident in that conversation was that God was working in a powerful way in this family and drawing a young man into a deeper sense of faith without what many would consider an orthodox Christian form of catechesis. This young man was growing and developing as a Christian despite the fact he was likely off the radar screen and certainly outside the context for much of what's considered youth ministry in some church traditions. This is becoming more and more the case. While the traditional models of church-based youth ministry continue to have a place, and parachurch ministries such as Young Life and Youth for Christ continue to make an impact, teens are also encountering God in meaningful ways outside of the church. This has been true throughout the centuries, but perhaps now more than ever it's important for those who work in youth ministry to humbly acknowledge and actively support alternatives to traditional youth ministries, rather than compete with them. As the lines blur between what's considered a Christian versus a non-Christian context for teens, so should those boundaries blur for parents, mentors, and church leaders.

To take this conversation further, it's helpful to reflect on the changing nature of society's understanding of what a teenager is and how culture is to contribute to the development of young people. Western culture is fixated upon what it means to be a teenager. The idolization of youth, the apparent limitlessness of life's possibilities, and the wonderful tension of adulthood and childhood blurring together all contribute to romanticism about and concern with what teens think, feel, and believe. Yet who teenagers *are* and who adults *think* teenagers should be is in itself in constant tension.

Should teens be fully realized adults once their bodies are mature? Should teens have as deep a grasp of the complexities of the Christian faith as their parents and the leaders of their faith communities do? Should we be concerned if teens can't articulate clear and concise faith statements by the time they reach junior high? High school? College? As media and mass culture moves faster and faster, it becomes harder to lock down what sources teenagers use to augment their ever-shifting notion of what it means to become an adult. This blurring of sources also makes it challenging for parents and leaders of faith communities to come up with a clear picture of teenagers in this fast-paced world. In the end much of the fixation on what a teenager is—or what adults think a teenager should be—makes it very difficult for most adults to track down and actually engage a teenager. Where are these teens? What are they thinking? What are they feeling? What social media outlets are they spending time on . . . and is it healthy?

In his seminal text on the history of adolescents in America titled *Rites of Passage: Adolescence in America 1790 to the Present*, Joseph Kett states:

> Those who measure the success of revolutions by their completeness will judge the revolution which has overtaken American young people in recent decades to be one of the most successful . . . They are essentially consumers rather than producers. Their contacts with adults are likely to occur in highly controlled environments such as the classroom, and the adults encountered are usually conveyors of specialized services such as education and guidance . . . [T]he economic and social relationship between youth and adults has clearly changed. Further, the change has been abrupt as well as been profound.[3]

This abrupt "change" in the relationship between adults and teens is in many ways the central concern of this book. What we hear in this quotation from Kett is that there's a growing chasm between the *perceptions* of who teenagers are and who they really are. Because of these rifts and because of our desire to better minister to generations that radically differ from our own, many church leaders have turned to quantitative studies such as Smith and Denton's now classic study of American teenagers in *Soul Searching*. The reason for this shift toward placing a high value upon social science research on how and why

---

3. Joseph Kett, *Rites of Passage: Adolescence in America 1790 to the Present* (New York: Basic Books, 1977), 3–4.

we do youth ministry is understandable and to be applauded. For far too long, much of what passed as youth ministry was primarily based on a desire to indoctrinate youth, rather than understand and engage them.

However, while such studies provide helpful data, they don't show the whole picture. There are blind spots in these studies that I will address in this book. As you'll see, I challenge the dominance of data-driven approaches to youth ministry because they lack an openness to the full—and often perplexing—story of what it means to be made in the image and likeness of God. This is what will be referred to as *blur*: a willingness to view teenagers in a way that embraces the complexities and paradoxes of coming of age in faith as a work in progress. It's my hope that rather than being concerned that teenagers lack clarity in their core faith statements and in many ways are on a journey to discover the height, breadth, and depth of a relationship with the God of the universe, you'll come to a place of grace, hope, and love for these teenagers whom God is raising up into a faith that's wild and mysterious and not the least bit boring or static.

The time has come for faith communities who love Jesus and trust God with our youth to reflect on youth culture through a lived, embodied, and fluid view of what it means to be human. With the rise of surveys and data-mining websites where adults can collect information about how teenagers think, what teenagers like to do, and where they like to spend their time, there's always the danger of seeing teenagers almost *too* objectively. At such a distance we can be left with a quantitative lens under which these young men and women are reduced to trends, attitudes, and fads rather than people with faces, names, hearts, and souls.

In an effort to quickly and efficiently assess and care for young people, there's a temptation to focus on finding the disease without asking what it means to be alive. St. Gregory of Nazianzus, one of the early church fathers, said Christians are known not by their sickness but by their cure. For us this can mean we don't watch for students to fall, but we invite them to run the race of faith with us by taking on Paul's challenge to fix our eyes on what lies ahead and run for it in a blur of motion and action. Just as the mother of that Boy Scout did, it's important that we step back and pay attention to where God is working in that moment and how young people are growing in faith and deepening their love for Jesus. If we do this, perhaps we can support rather than compete with the culture in those moments. Working with young people will always mean moving into the confusing, yet-to-be-fully understood world they inhabit—but we're to do it with the right spirit.[4]

This was always made clear to me during my first meetings with parents and volunteers in the youth program at the beginning of the new school year. When I was a youth director, it was during this meeting that I would outline the various Sunday school themes and texts we'd be studying, the programs and themes we'd be focusing on in Wednesday night youth group, the various outreach and mission activities we were planning, and the ways in which we hoped parents and other adults in the church could be actively involved.

The youth ministry I was involved in at one point was at a midsized church in a middle- and upper-middle-class area. Many of the parents in this congregation had an image of youth ministry as being a safe space where teenagers would always be

---

4. Part of this task will entail dialogue with a subdiscipline of theology called "practical theology" that has broadened its scope beyond what theologian Edward Farley has termed a "comprehensive paradigm." While keeping central its task of training and equipping clergy and others who work for and within the church, it also seeks to look toward active critical reflection, moving beyond the world of management and skill acquisition to understanding the church in the world itself.

engaged with clearly outlined social and intellectual markers to know what a Christian was supposed to be. Of course these are wonderful expectations, and certainly this was part of my vision of youth ministry as well. Yet more often than not, there would always be one or two parents during the question-and-answer time who would ask something to the effect of, "One of the concerns I have is that my child is [listening/watching/reading/etc.] too much secular [music/movies/videos/books/magazines/etc.]. I wondered if you have any suggestions for Christian [music/movies/videos/books/magazines/etc.] that I should be encouraging [him/her] to [listen/watch/read/etc.] instead." Let me be clear: I've been blessed by the ministry, artistry, and creative vision of many artists who are faithful followers of Jesus. But what was often behind this question was an assumption about youth ministry being a place to indoctrinate and ultimately protect and separate one's child from the *secular* world. There's an idea that if the church doesn't teach young people to be very critical—and at times fearful—of the culture around them, then like sailors called by the beguiling sirens in Homer's *Odyssey*, teenagers will be drawn away from God and toward certain destruction.

When I first started in youth ministry, I felt this anxiety. So in response, I'd exclusively play contemporary Christian music, direct the youth to books with overtly Christian themes, and watch films with them that, if not overtly Christian, were at least easily understood within a Christian moral and cultural framework. What I found was that while I was trying to tie the youth group to the mast of Christian media, God was showing up in these teenagers' friends' secular music, books, magazines, and videos. The result was that my students found themselves living in two worlds, where the world of the church and youth group was a foreign country with a different language, customs, and holiday traditions.

So when parents asked, "Do you have suggestions for Christian [music/movies/videos/books/magazines/etc.] that I should be encouraging my child to [listen/watch/read/etc.]," I began providing tools to help them see that God is continually blurring the lines of what's sacred and secular; that certainty of faith and what deepens faith may be different at times; and that the aspects of our culture that are mysterious, wild, and out of our control may not be scary and dangerous after all. Another way to say this is that in order to truly minister to teenagers, we need to engage the culture in which they're being formed and deepened: we need to listen to the beats of their music; actively watch the videos they celebrate; read the fantasy novels that awaken their imaginations; ask why tattoos and piercings are profound and—at times—sacramental experiences; discuss the challenges and possibilities of the educational system that occupies much of their waking lives; and delve into the complexities of race, economics, status, and ethnicity that frame the bodies, minds, and souls of these young people. With opened eyes, ears, and hearts, we may find that God is doing so much more in teenagers' lives than we thought.

HOW WE TALK ABOUT YOUTH IS OFTEN HOW WE EXPERIENCE YOUTH

The question of how young people grow into a sustainable faith is at the forefront of many faith communities' concerns, and it needs our collective cultural attention. Various resources produced over the past few years have leaned heavily on data to back up ministry practice and effectiveness, and 2012 marked the ten-year anniversary of the first wave of data collected by the National Study of Youth and Religion (NSYR).[5] As

---

5. The NSYR continues to update its findings online at www.youthandreligion. org/research and has been incredibly generous with sharing its findings.

many church leaders and youth workers in America can attest, this study (which sociologists Christian Smith and Melinda Lundquist Denton published in 2005 as *Soul Searching*[6]) has been profound.

The NSYR began its work as a representative survey of U.S. households in forty-five states with teenagers between the ages of thirteen and seventeen, and it progressed to include qualitative in-person interviews with 267 representative teens from across the country. The NSYR offered the cumulative view that young people in America were developing not as orthodox to their respective faith traditions *per se*, but rather into Moralistic Therapeutic Deists. According to Smith and Denton, teenagers view God as a means for discerning right and wrong ethical behavior (moralistic); believe God has a central and primary concern for the individual needs of the self prior to those of a community (therapeutic); and see God as ultimately distant from the day-to-day activities of our lives, usually only interceding in times of crisis, if at all (deism). This distilled rendering of the NSYR into the catch phrase "Moralistic Therapeutic Deism (MTD)" has become so commonplace in many faith communities that it's hard to remember a time when teenagers were thought of in any other way. Even in faith communities that are unfamiliar with the specifics of the NSYR, the implications of the study often affect the way in which youth ministry is carried out. The concern that young people are neither talking about nor living out faith in ways that are considered traditional, let alone orthodox, is something that's been around for centuries. And every age must address the changing means by which the next generation takes up the mantle of the faith and builds bridges into the future. I've shared with some other theologians that what's needed isn't necessarily more clarity

---

6. Cf. Christian Smith and Melinda Lundquist Denton, *Soul Searching: The Religious and Spiritual Lives of American Teenagers* (New York: Oxford University Press, 2009).

from the youth who contribute to the NSYR report on faith, but perhaps more mystery, wonder, and awe.

As we review Christian Smith's trilogy, *Soul Searching, Souls in Transition*, and *Lost in Transition*, as well as Lisa Pearce and Melinda Lundquist Denton's *A Faith of Their Own*,[7] we can see in the first three waves of the NYSR[8] that the outcomes point to the complexity of teenagers' faith journeys, yet also sound a note of alarm. The result is that faith communities who receive this data frequently respond with fear rather than hope. In large part this is due to a basic reality that anyone working directly with young people will tell you: the future that teens desire and the resources through which they encounter and deepen their Christian faith is often not in sync with the pasts of their parents and youth leaders. Language, images, and metaphors all shift and change with the culture and so, too, do the means by which young people discover and affirm what faith will be.

As Scripture has moved from scrolls to books to apps, what it means to merely read and engage the Word of God has dramatically changed. Images that represent faith have moved from being fixed images on canvas and stained glass to CGI and flash animation. People find community in virtual as well as physical locations, and the space between them is a blurred continuum of meaning-making where the online conversations spill over seamlessly into face-to-face encounters. Sometimes this is cause for concern, but it's also a cause for hopefulness and inspiration.

---

7. Lisa D. Pearce and Melinda Lundquist Denton, *A Faith of Their Own: Stability and Change in the Religiosity of America's Adolescents* (New York: Oxford University Press, 2011).

8. The third wave of NSYR surveys was completed in 2008 following up with the initial interview group as they progressed into young adulthood. It was published in 2009 by Christian Smith and Patricia Snell as *Souls in Transition: The Religious and Spiritual Lives of Emerging Adults* (New York: Oxford University Press, 2009) and the recent Christian Smith et. al., *Lost in Transition: The Dark Side of Emerging Adulthood* (New York: Oxford University Press, 2011).

In regard to developing ways of raising up new communities of youth in deep faith formation, these shifts in how young people read, see, meet, and experience community also mean that how we'll locate what it means to grow into faith will be a bit blurry at times—not as fixed and easily discernible as some might think. The ways in which we measure faith in young people will be limited if we're more concerned with a measurable assessment of religious tradition literacy than a robust faith formation filled with wonder and ineffable engagement with mystery.

It's this call to work from a place of promise, hope, mystery, and wonder that has evolved into *Blur*. This book is intended for youth workers who've engaged or hope to engage teenagers in the blurring of boundaries that's contemporary youth culture. Rather than dismiss the important findings of the NSYR research, *Blur* offers some further depth and movement toward a critical conversation[9] that draws together how we respond to young people in all aspects of their lives—not merely how they answer fixed questions that lack the flexibility and paradox found in real lives. I am hopeful that this will allow a richer and more robust view into the blur of youth culture, the young people we love, and the God who loves them.

BONHOEFFER AND CANTUS FIRMUS: FAITH AS MUSIC THAT BLURS INTO DISSONANT AND HARMONIOUS UNITY

One way to frame this dynamic approach to faith formation in the midst of the blur of youth culture is through resources such as art, music, literature, and poetry that are often used to exemplify

---

9. See Stephen Pattison, "Some Straw for the Bricks" in *The Blackwell Reader in Pastoral and Practical Theology* (London: Wiley-Blackwell, 2000), 135–148. A *critical conversation* is a move into a pastoral space where all parties are willing to change and learn as the result of the encounter.

theological and doctrinal core beliefs. Youth are formed by the culture in which they exist, and the ways in which churches and youth workers have distilled and brokered the results of the NSYR data has only heightened the fearful call for expressly Christian culture in many sectors. Yet seeking to grow teenagers' faith through this isolated Christian subculture results in stunted and anxious teenagers who become petrified of the world that John 3:16 tells us Christ died for. In Dietrich Bonhoeffer's *Letters and Papers from Prison*, we hear an appeal drawn from his engagement with music for a dynamic model of faith formation:

> 20 May 1944
>
> There's always a danger in all strong, erotic love that one may love what I might call the polyphony of life. What I mean is that God wants us to love him eternally with our whole hearts—not in such a way as to injure or weaken our earthly love, but to provide a kind of *cantus firmus* to which the other melodies of life provide the counterpoint. One of these contrapuntal themes (which have their own complete independence but are yet related to the *cantus firmus*) is earthly affection. Even in the Bible we have the Song of Songs; and really one can imagine no more ardent, passionate, sensual love than is portrayed there . . . It's a good thing that the book is in the Bible, in face of all those who believe that the restraint of passion is Christian (where is there such restraint in the Old Testament?). Where the *cantus firmus* is clear and plain, the counterpoint can be developed to its limits. The two are 'undivided and yet distinct,' in the words of the Chalcedonian Definition, like Christ in his divine and human natures. May not the attraction and importance of polyphony in music consist in its being a musical reflection of this Christological fact and therefore of our *vita christiana*? This thought didn't occur to me till after your visit yesterday. Do you see what I'm driving at? I wanted to tell you to have a good, clear *cantus firmus*; that is the only way to a full and perfect sound, when the counterpoint has a firm support and can't come adrift or get out of tune, while remaining a distinct whole in its own right. Only a polyphony of this kind can give life a wholeness and at the same time assure us that nothing calamitous can happen as long as

the *cantus firmus* is kept going. Perhaps a good deal will be easier
to bear in these days together, and possibly also in the days ahead
when you're separated. Please, Eberhard, do not fear and hate the
separation, if it should come again with all its dangers, but rely on
the *cantus firmus*—I don't know whether I've made myself clear
now, but one so seldom speaks of such things . . . [10]

Here Bonhoeffer is developing a fascinating aesthetic theology of personhood in this short letter around this ancient musical principle of the *cantus firmus*. A *cantus firmus* is a melody to which can be added one or more contrapuntal parts—parts that are truly distinct, novel, and even seemingly at odds with other parts until they are bound to this consistent yet fluid melody that is the *cantus firmus*. Bonhoeffer extends the music analogy to the Christian life by stating that the arc of the *cantus firmus* is similar to our relationality to the triune God who is the core melody of our lives that carries and propels the contrapuntal parts toward a note a step above the final. This drive toward a final point is a point of no return (think Galatians 2:20: "I no longer live, but Christ lives in me") that catalyzes into a climax on a high note, which is in harmony with the first and final notes, creating unity from the first to the last.[11] Throughout the movement there's always modulation and balance that allows space for variation, change, innovation—even dissonance. If the *cantus firmus* is heard, then diversity is not only tolerable, but also celebratory given its allegiance to the core musical theme. If the *cantus firmus* is dampened—think of white noise generators in Bose headphones—then order is sought through an external locus of control for fear of chaos and anarchy.

What would it mean for work with young people to be

---

10. Dietrich Bonhoeffer, *Letters and Papers from Prison. Updated Version* (New York: Touchstone, 1997) 162–3.

11. I.e., such as the distance of a major or minor 3rd, perfect 4th or 5th, major or minor 6th, perfect 8ve, or major or minor 10th.

considered a method in harmony with Bonhoeffer's understanding of the *cantus firmus*? As Bonhoeffer alludes in this description of the power of music where different and dissonant voices can find common ground, so too should the church be a place where a variety of voices can find places around the cross that don't require only one way of articulating what it means to have faith. Much like in Acts 2 when the Holy Spirit descended like fire upon the gathered believers and allowed many different languages to be understood, so, too, can we allow for youth to gather with fiery passion around the cross without needing to have only one language of faith.

W. B. YEATS' "AMONG SCHOOL CHILDREN": WHEN DOES THE DANCER BECOME THE DANCE?

So much of what constitutes Christian formation in young people can degenerate into managing chaos through control in the guise of a search for certainty in an uncertain world. Henri Nouwen in his book *Creative Ministry* states it in the following way:

> "Getting things under control" is what keeps most teachers and students busy, and a successful teacher is often the individual who creates the conviction that humans have the necessary tools to tame the dangerous lion they will face as soon as they leave the training field. *As long as teaching takes place in this context, it is doomed to be a violent process and evoke a vicious cycle of action and reaction in which we face our world as new territory that has to be conquered but is filled with enemies unwilling to be ruled by a stranger.* The teacher who enters this arena is forced to enter into a process which by its nature is competitive, unilateral, and alienating. *In short: violent.*[12] (emphasis added)

---

12. Henri Nouwen, *Creative Ministry*, Revised ed. (New York: Random House, 2003), 11–12.

How often does work with young people become a competitive, unilateral, and alienating experience—especially if our posture is one of fear of their culture coupled with a lack of faith in who they already are in the image of God? In William Butler Yeats' poem *Among School Children*, the sixty-year-old schoolteacher narrating the poem muses about the development of youth as he "walk[s] through the long schoolroom questioning" while the children "learn to cipher and to sing, /To study reading-books and histories, /To cut and sew, be neat in everything/In the best modern way."[13] As the youth sit fixed on their studies, the aging protagonist laments what he sees and wonders if these youth are being taught what it means to be alive in the world.

And as he reflects on his own life, this aged teacher remembers that there came a day when it seemed that "our two natures blent /Into a sphere from youthful sympathy, /Or else, to alter Plato's parable, /Into the yolk and white of the one shell." The irony that he points to is that the great people whom the young people are studying in a context of control and stillness were once young people themselves, full of imagination, with fire in their bellies for change, and captivated by the mystery in life. They had a willingness to dig ever deeper for meaning even while they were uncertain as to what or who they were searching for. As the protagonist leaves the children in the schoolroom, he wonders to the classroom, "Are you the leaf, the blossom or the bole? /O body swayed to music, O brightening glance, /How can we know the dancer from the dance?"

Yeats' summative question—"How can we know the dancer from the dance?"—is a reminder that for those of us working alongside youth, our concern ultimately is to acknowledge that human development is often a generative blur of fully living out our identity with other disciples of faith. It should challenge us

---

13. W. B. Yeats, "Among School Children" in *The Collected Poems of W.B. Yeats*, ed. Richard J. Finneran, rev. 2nd edition (New York: Scribner's, 1996), 215.

with three organizing opportunities—three ways to encourage fluidity in both our approach to ministry and what we expect from young people as they live out the dance of faith: (1) Ministry to and with youth should have the primary concern of equipping today's young people for mobility and depth, counter to the prevailing trend in youth ministry that argues for fixity and certainty in place and belief. (2) The destabilizing nature of identity formation (as we'll look at in more depth in chapter 3) should be engaged with the aesthetic nature of culture, which allows for fluidity of self in concert with divine action (something that lasts and endures beyond the plastic and temporal call to clear definitions of faith). (3) Deep and abiding Christian formation of young people requires a renewed emphasis upon the *form* of being[14] in relation to the *content* of being—that is to say, a return to discipleship as transforming and not merely informing youth. Here I think of the theological anthropology found in St. Augustine of Hippo and in particular his work *Confessions*, which provides a call to recognize the fluidity of youth formation found in the inner movement of deep identity and memory grounded in the saving power of Jesus Christ. To this end, Augustine provides a compelling response to Yeats' quandary by taking *Confessions* to "the dance floor,"[15] as it were—our inner and outer lives as

---

14. Here I am seeking to deepen the doctrine of theological anthropology to see what it means to be a human being as truly bound to a study of "who is God?" (theology) and "what are human beings that God is mindful of them?" (Psalm 8:4 as anthropology). In this way the study of human beings as creatures made "in the image of God" (Genesis 1:27) we see that we are made for communion with God and each other, living under the judgment because of our sin, living under the mercy of God because of Jesus Christ.

15. To the pop culturally astute, the reference to the title of Madonna's 2005 album *Confessions on a Dance Floor* is intentional with the corrective of the definitive article. Where Madonna is careful to acknowledge through the employment of the indefinite article that her dance floor is merely one of many dance floors in our pluralistic world, I argue along with Augustine that there is but one ground for authentic being *the* dance floor where we all join the dance whether we're part of the pulsing mosh pit or we're passive wallflowers on the fringe.

theological dance partners that when in synchronic movement in and with the social Trinity of Father, Son, and Holy Spirit provide youth a rhythm and trajectory in the task of becoming deep and abiding disciples.

As I've suggested throughout this chapter and will repeat as a core theme throughout the book, youth workers can make an error in seeing today's youth culture as a search for fixity over and against mobility. I not only wish to share the potential of what a young person can be, but I also want to issue a challenge to let go of our need to know for certain what a young person believes. Instead, we should concentrate on who they are, where they exist in their culture, and why they are the way they are. By doing this perhaps we won't be so fearful of the world, nor be so quick to pull them away from the context in which God may be developing them into the disciples he wishes them to be.

The task before us in working with teenagers is to encourage experiences that seek depth of being where mobility and change is a gift rather than a developmental deficit to be overcome. In this way we can help teenagers see what it means to be moved by the initiative of God's calling regardless of cultural location. Whether God is growing and shaping a young person in a youth group ministry or in the midst of an indie rock concert isn't a concern as long as we're willing to support him or her on the journey and God is there.

As I'll discuss in the chapters to come, teenagers often exhibit a strength in their faith that comes from being constantly mobile in a secularized culture, because neither locale nor environment is viewed as a primary source by which identity is to be formed. Because of constantly moving in and out of cultures, teenagers not only have to learn new cultural rules, but, more fundamentally, they must understand who they are in relationship to—and at times despite—the surrounding culture(s).

CHAPTER 2

BLURRING CULTURE(S)

Accelerated Cultures and Faith Formation
through Conviction, Character,
and Community

I recently attended a baptismal service for two middle schoolers from my daughter's youth group. The service was held at a lake near our church on a beautiful sunny day, and many of the teens' friends from youth group attended, as well as family members and church members of all ages. The young people standing around talking and laughing before the service began represented a blur on multiple levels: they were young people of different ethnic, economic, cultural, and denominational backgrounds. Since this event was held at a public park, there were a number of other people gathered on the beach and in the water. I knew most of the young people in the youth group, so I knew which young people were there for the service and which ones just happened to be in the water for swimming.

Yet if you were to just use external cues, it would be difficult to separate the group of church teens from the rest. The clothing styles for all of the young people at the lake that day ran the gamut: trucker hats, board shorts, skinny jeans, and tank tops with various logos. The music blaring from Bluetooth speakers on the picnic tables was a mixture in the wind of dance tracks, Americana, hip-hop, old-school emo, and straight-edge punk.

As I watched the church youth standing around and talking, moving a bit when they picked up a beat to a song they recognized, and waving at friends across the park, I realized how difficult it has become to determine at a glance who are the churched and who are the unchurched. These young people were gathered for various reasons, yet they were drawing identity from so many similar sources found in popular culture, I was reminded again of how sacredly mobile they were. They were dancing around, laughing, waving at one another, moving into the water for baptism or for a nice swim—yet all were in the same waters, all of them were moving and growing in their understanding of life, identity, and the presence of God. The love of God surrounded all of them in different ways by supporting them, growing the grass beneath their feet, pouring sunshine upon all of them equally, and creating the waters of life that lapped the shoreline and called to baptism those who were ready. What was abundantly clear was the flow of culture moving and swirling around all of us—the sights and sounds of mass media were literally in the air. But, in many ways, this was exactly as it should be. The line between those young people was simply a blurred one. What wasn't blurred was who they all were in Christ, how much God loved them all, and how each and every one of those young people were products of the same desires to have their lives mean more than merely living and dying. We can see this on a microscale like this park scene, yet we can also see this on a macro global scale as well.

Since September 11, much has been made of Samuel Huntington's *The Clash of Civilizations and the Remaking of World Order* and the global blurring of preconceived cultural boundaries on multiple levels: ethnic, economic, etc.[16] As opposed to a clash of cultures, youth culture has become a "mash-up" of cultures drawing on diverse sources for meaning-making—often without critical reflection or discrimination.

This mash-up—or what I'm calling the "blur" of cultural identity formation—often takes place outside of traditional institutions such as school and church through what Arjun Appadurai calls the *global cultural economy*. The instantaneous dissemination of electronic images and sounds provides fantastic resources that invigorate the imagination and transform everyday discourse. Appadurai states, "neither images nor viewers fit into circuits or audiences that are easily bound within local, national, or regional spaces."[17] And throughout the world youth culture is remarkably similar: youth recognize each other beyond once meaningful cultural boundaries through their shared music, film, body art, and the like. Boundaries aren't entirely breaking down, but they are certainly becoming more fluid or very, very blurred.

This was evident at the lakeside that day as I watched all of those young people. Clearly the public did not see those young people as churched versus unchurched kids. Is this a problem? For some people the point of youth ministry is to have teens set apart from what is termed "the world," which is seen as distinct from the church. But young people are bound into the world because Christ has reconciled the world to himself. As such, youth will always be a part of the cultures they come from and live into.

The Zandl Group, a consulting research group specializing in young consumer trends, maintains a nationwide panel of

16. Samuel Huntington, *The Clash of Civilizations and the Remaking of World Order* (New York: Simon and Schuster, 1998).

17. Arjun Appadurai, *Modernity at Large: Cultural Dimensions of Globalization* (Minneapolis and London: University of Minnesota Press, 1996), 4.

more than 3,000 young people, ages eight to twenty-four, in order to stay in touch with youth trends on an ongoing basis. The HotSheet produced by the Zandl Group is similar to many other high-end reviews of culture that marketing firms offer to companies looking for important trends in youth culture. My purpose in listing some of these findings is not to endorse nor denounce them but give a picture of the world in which many teenagers find themselves. Some of these might seem dated since trends change so rapidly (much faster than a book can be published!); but it does give a snapshot of the world in which teens live and breathe.

Some recent findings include the following:

1. While there is a growing suspicion of "otherness" in Western culture and a move toward the hegemonic, the otherness of different cultures is compelling, not frightening, for today's youth:

    One in ten young Americans today is of Hispanic descent, and this number is on the rise. With its roots in the Hispanic street scene, Hispanic street culture has an authenticity and edginess comparable to hip-hop culture as a creative, communal force that's compelling for mainstream young people. Hispanic culture has influenced music (Pitbull, Shakira), TV (Mun2 TV Network), and entertainment (Selena Gomez, Demi Lovato, Zoe Saldana, Sofia Vergara).

    Driven by manga (Japanese comic books), anime (movie and television animation), and video games, Asian pop culture continues to be a continuously pervasive force in youth culture globally. Asian culture is considered normative including cuisine (sushi) and beverages (bubble tea), spirituality of well-being (meditation, Zen) and fitness (yoga, martial arts in movies), the face of technology (the "cool" factor of hybrid cars and smart houses), art (manga), and spectator sports (drifting, Japanese sumo wrestling). Anime

and action figures created for adults are changing perceptions of cartoons (many of the the Cartoon Network and
Adult Swim's features are anime) and toys, and the modern
vibe of cities like Tokyo, Hong Kong, and Shanghai continues to influence advertising, music videos, and Hollywood
movies.

2. Gender identity has become more challenging as the mark-
    ers of what is male and female continue to blur:

    A new post-feminist generation is redefining what it
    means to be male and female. Girls continue to participate
    in domains that were traditionally male: playing football,
    lifting weights, playing video games, driving fast cars, and
    street racing. Women rockers, liberated urban dwellers
    (from *Sex and the City* to HBO's *Girls*), power players (real-
    ity shows like *The Apprentice*), and action heroines in films
    and television have become powerful icons in the entertain-
    ment world. The number of women who graduate from col-
    lege outnumber the guys; and 25 percent of married women
    now earn more than their husbands do, which is starting to
    change the way many teens think about homemaking and
    parenting.

3. Modesty and morality have shifted to being cool:

    Although explicit sexuality and skimpy clothing are still
    a part of youth culture, research shows that young people
    are getting tired of the prevailing cultural vibe (aggres-
    sive, subversive, sleazy), and they are seeking an antidote
    in things that please the eye instead of assaulting it. This
    emerging counter-trend may be seen in beauty ideals (the
    natural look), fashion (understated), hip-hop style that is
    buttoned-up, music videos that are tame (stars as diverse
    as Taylor Swift, Björk, and Westlife continue to offer up
    music videos that are not sexually explicit), and holis-
    tic retail environments (Whole Foods). The Paleo Diet is

gaining popularity, and being vegan is not considered odd. On television, the popularity of makeover shows that transform people's style (*Say Yes to the Dress*, *What Not to Wear*) reflects the desire to make the world a more beautiful place. Apple is still a company that delivers beauty in its product design, retail stores, and advertising—and young people are responding as iPhones and iPads continue to offer style as well as function.

4. Interest in spirituality:

One of the most interesting discoveries regarding youth consumer culture has been the acknowledgment that today's preteens and teens are deeply concerned about the question of God. Involvement with spirituality and religion has been growing for several years, but it has been under the media's radar. Now, with the rising awareness of Islam; the same-sex marriage debate dominating the nightly news; and politicians, celebrities, and pro athletes openly wearing their faith on their sleeves, spirituality and morality have become part of the zeitgeist. It's a theme in books whether they are expressly Christian (*Love Wins*, *Blue Like Jazz*, *Crazy Love*) or literary fiction that grounds its conversations in questions of God (Chaim Potok's *The Chosen*, Yann Martel's *Life of Pi*, Laurie Halse Anderson's historical YA novels *Chains* and *Forge*), TV shows that deal with the moral complexity of our time (*Pretty Little Liars*), as well as taking questions of the supernatural on board as a road to consider the transcendent (*Twilight*, *Teen Wolf*, *Game of Thrones*), satire that points to big questions requiring deep reflection (*The Daily Show*, *South Park*, *Family Guy*), and the continued growth of contemporary Christian music in the mainstream. Young people are actively affirming their faith in open ways, from church youth groups to prayer circles with their friends.

In short, youth today are seeking sources to bring meaning to their lives, and this can provide incredible insight for shaping a robust youth ministry program. The teens who populate church youth groups are drawing insights and resourcing their faith from popular culture: the songs they listen to, the movies and videos they watch with friends, and the links they share in social media. What this offers those of us who work with youth is an opportunity not to fear what the culture is offering teenagers, but to acknowledge that God is very much involved in the lives of teens—within the community of faith as well as outside of it.

Let's go back to our view of teens as sacredly mobile: To see teens as *sacred* is to begin our work with them with faith that God is at work in their lives before we meet them, that God is stirring up evidence of his grace in ways both profound and at times seemingly mundane, that the Lord is calling and awakening young people to the common grace found in the creation that Jesus redeemed and reconciled on the cross, and that teenagers don't have to leave behind everything in the culture in order to be a faithful follower of Christ. This is an acknowledgment of their *mobility* as well—they will change and move in and out of sources that God will bring to bear in relationships, culture, and opportunities for spiritual insight that will not be easily discerned at times and will be what Eugene Peterson once defined as discipleship: "a long obedience in the same direction."[18] One thing the NSYR underscores in its research that's vitally important to remember is that young people crave the example and intimacy of key adult leaders in their lives. According to the data of the NSYR, parents and faith community leaders are still the number one influencer for teens when it comes to their developing a robust faith. As we consider

---

18. Eugene Peterson, *A Long Obedience in the Same Direction: Discipleship in an Instant Society* (Downers Grove, IL: InterVarsity Press, 2000).

what it means to navigate mass youth culture as it shifts around us, we must remember that we're still called to walk alongside teens—this means even when they travel outside of what we might see as the boundaries of faith. This is where mentors become so very important in young people's lives to assist them in interpreting the culture, grounding their experiences in a larger context of faith, and journeying with them to explore and deeply experience the ways God is reaching out to them.

In his book *The Fabric of Faithfulness: Weaving Together Belief and Behavior*, Steven Garber states that young people who make the move from a statement of personal faith toward a life of character-formed action in the world are "taught a worldview . . . sufficient for the questions and crises of the next twenty years, particularly the challenge of modern and postmodern consciousness with its implicit secularization and pluralization."[19] As we see throughout Scripture, the importance of teaching and modeling for youth the central tenets of the Christian faith isn't optional. Terry McGonigal at Whitworth University has made this clear in relation to youth evangelism:

> Biblically speaking, youth are linked with the stage of childhood when dependence upon parents and community for life support, nurture, guidance, and instruction is the rule. The terms *child* and *children* are mentioned quite frequently in the Old Testament—over 550 times. The community of God's people is given special responsibility to care for the children.[20]

To love God fully is to impress this love upon the lives of the next generation—this is core to loving God with all of our

---

19. Steven Garber, *The Fabric of Faithfulness: Weaving Together Belief and Behavior*, Expanded edition (Downers Grove, IL: InterVarsity Press, 2007), 51.

20. Terry McGonigal, "Focusing Youth Ministry through Evangelism" in Kenda Creasy Dean, Chap Clark, and Dave Rahn (eds.), *Starting Right: Thinking Theologically about Youth Ministry* (Grand Rapids, MI: Zondervan, 2001), 126.

hearts, minds, souls, and strength. In this way, our conviction needs to be made tangible for youth so they are included in the journey with us—a move from mere transmission of dogma to embodied praxis and pilgrimage.[21]

What binds these together is a call to share with others the vital and animating parts of our lives of faith. St. Augustine said we'll love that which is loved by the people we love most. In order for young people to become convicted, we must risk drawing close to them in intimate and trustworthy relationships so they might experience that which convicts us.

BUILDING CHARACTER THROUGH KNOWLEDGE

Garber states that those young people who make the shift from belief to behavior are most often those who "met a teacher [or mentor] who incarnated the worldview which they were coming to consciously identify as their own, and in and through that relationship they saw that it was possible to reside within that worldview themselves."[22] In short, Garber advocates what Stanley Hauerwas in *A Community of Character*, Sharon Daloz Parks in *The Critical Years* and *Common Fire*, as well as more straight-ahead youth ministry monographs such as Thomas Bergler's recent *The Juvenilization of American Christianity*,[23] Dean Borgman's *Hear My Story*, and Chap Clark's *Hurt: Inside the World of Today's Teenagers*[24] have argued as well: character is something actively modeled in the lives of mentor fig-

---

21. See Ian Bradley, *Colonies of Heaven: Celtic Models for Today's Church* (London: Dartman, Longman & Todd, 2000), especially pp. 197–244.

22. Garber, *The Fabric of Faithfulness*, 51.

23. Thomas E. Bergler, *The Juvenilization of American Christianity* (Grand Rapids, MI: Eerdmans, 2012).

24. See Chap Clark, *Hurt: Inside the World of Today's Teenagers* (Grand Rapids, MI: Baker Academic, 2004).

ures before and with youth—not a reasoned ethical construct offered at a distance.

The result of youth abandonment in an accelerated culture results in many of the horrors that continue to disturb us—the most notable being the recent re-imaginings of the Columbine shootings in award-winning movies and novels as the definitive metaphor of youth culture today. Part of the response to the events of Columbine has been a renewed assertion of the importance of character as part of the educational process. With the recent legislative moves toward curricular reform, character education has moved from being suggested to mandatory in all fifty states.

The days of creating polarizing relationships with public schools need to be put to rest. There's a real opportunity in youth ministry to train leaders who are involved with youth to understand the states' curriculum standards and provide a role in helping schools meet the character standards in exciting ways. Here's a grand opportunity to work together with public schools as fellow educators in actualizing real and sustained change. Where parachurch organizations have for far too long underscored that they are prevented from doing ministry in schools, which adds an "outsider" identity to their ministries, it's time for those who are concerned with schools and the world that young people live and learn in to become partners in new and exciting ways. For example, I encourage my students who are training for youth ministry to download the school curriculum from the school district website. Using the required reading and outcome lists, these youth ministry students develop curriculum based on junior and senior high humanities courses that allows them to build a bridge between the classrooms to world of the faith.

It's shocking how many youth workers have never asked the teenagers they're serving what books they're reading and what key topics they're wrestling with. Learning has been a spiritual discipline of the church since the rise of the monastic movement in the fourth century. According to Thomas Aquinas, all knowledge has an element of common grace and is useful for the deepening of the faith. To engage the learning of our students is an act of deep character building that puts the world of knowledge in a moral context that will have lasting and incarnational meaning.

THE NEED FOR COMMUNITY

Garber made the discovery that the young people in his study were more likely to bridge the gap from belief to behavior when they made choices regarding their worldview "in the company of mutually committed folk who provided a network of stimulation and support which showed that the ideas could be coherent across the whole of life."[25] Three things that exemplify this focus on community are important to remember as we discuss the blurring nature of youth identity formation in later chapters:

1. A continued shifting nature of what's meant by "family":

    There's still quite a bit of work to do in moving critical reflection on youth culture beyond the paradigm of coming of age as merely a struggle to differentiate from the traditional family unit. Studies from the 1960s continue to shape the contemporary imagination and rhetoric concerning youth in crisis. Consider the following passage from an article published in 1964:

    > The adolescent presumably is engaged in a struggle to emancipate himself from his parents. He therefore resists and rebels against any restrictions and controls they impose upon his behavior.[26]

---

25. Garber, *The Fabric of Faithfulness*, 52.
26. Albert Bandura, "The Stormy Decade: Fact or Fiction," *Psychology in the Schools* 1(3) (July 1964), 224-231.

Today we have an opportunity to correct and directly assess one of the current misunderstandings of the key factors driving youth development in America. As Chap Clark has correctly assessed, youth aren't primarily battling parental restrictions and boundaries these days; instead, they've been "abandoned" by their role models. This means they no longer have what David Elkind in *All Grown Up and No Place to Go* termed critical "markers" for what it means to be growing and developing into holistic adults.[27] Family has been and continues to be one of the great challenges and opportunities for ministry to youth—both to strengthen the existing family units, and provide authentic markers *in loco parentis* or "in place of the parents" where the family unit has come under crisis. This is certainly one of the great services youth ministry provides not only to the church, but also to the culture at large.

I see this more and more as I work with public school teachers. One of the courses I regularly teach is in the graduate school of education for K-12 teachers seeking models for literacy education and moral/character education to integrate into the state-standard curriculum. As I work with these teachers, they're always amazed at the level of engagement many youth pastors and youth directors have relating to curriculum planning, project management, and community organizing. More and more of them are looking for assistance in the classroom and in the community in order to fulfill their mission as holistic educators. And some of

---

27. David Elkind, *All Grown Up and No Place to Go: Teenagers in Crisis* (Reading, PA: Addison-Wesley, 1984). As Elkind states on page 93, "markers" serve as external signs of where we stand "in the stages on life's way . . . 'Markers' protect teenagers by helping them attain a clear self-definition, and they reduce stress by supplying rules, limits, taboos, and prohibitions that liberate teenagers from the need to make age-appropriate decisions and choices."

the most qualified people to help them are youth directors in churches and parachurch organizations.

2. Opportunities for real-time/face-to-face contact amidst an ever-accelerated world:

As more and more relational activities occur in the virtual realm, there will be an ever-increasing need for opportunities to experience relational growth, emotional joys, and disappointments. In her book *Life on the Screen: Identity in the Age of the Internet*, MIT professor Sherry Turkle makes the following point: "[O]nce we take virtuality seriously as a way of life, we need a new language for talking about the simplest things. Each individual must ask: What is the nature of my relationships? What are the limits of my responsibility? And even more basic: Who and what am I?"[28] While the virtual realm provides a level of personal reflection and growth that ultimately can't be sustained in real life and can hamper growth and intimacy, it also can be a space and medium for deep connection if we engage young people in the midst of such arenas with authentic and vulnerable connection.

Where the virtual realm insists upon an ever-accelerated pace, the charge for contemporary youth ministry is not to do more and do it faster. Rather, we should do less at a more

28. Sherry Turkle, *Life on the Screen: Identity in the Age of the Internet* (New York: Simon and Schuster, 1997), 15. Turkle makes the observation that with networked computers, people are creating alternative identities, forming disembodied relationships, and building imaginary places that are beginning to interest and involve us as much as those in the physical world. As youth spend more time in the Mac and Windows platform interfaces—which allow us to run several applications at once, cycling among different work and play identities throughout the day—this encourages youth to think of our minds and selves as multiple and decentralized. Turkle states that rather than having a Luddite response to technology, these changes can have positive effects—but only if we're willing to accept that they're already happening and be thoughtful in deciding what we wish to do with them. We must be aware of how computer-mediated relationships work if we want to optimize the human side of the relationship.

human speed—yet still acknowledge that we can be human in the midst of a tethered world. (This will be explored more in chapter 5.) The challenge for young people is to see models of tempered and intentional media and technology management. The encouragement to take a tech Sabbath each week is just one way youth leaders can model a good and faithful relationship with technology for the sake of deeper relationships in community.

3. Community as an ever-expanding engagement with reconciliation in and with the world around us:

Cheryl Sanders in her book *Ministry at the Margins: The Prophetic Mission of Women, Youth and the Poor* makes the following assertion with regard to the importance of reconciliation surrounding the issue of racial and ethnic diversity in the world that today's youth "live and move and have their being":

> The gospel of Jesus Christ is meaningless without reconciliation. . . . The ministry of reconciliation is fundamental to the Christian faith. It is no accident that the Spirit chose an international, multicultural gathering of believers in Jerusalem as the setting for the Pentecost outpouring, whose testimony was that "in our own languages we hear them speaking about God's deeds of power" (Acts 2:11). Pentecost is God's remedy for disunity. Many languages, many colors, many cultures, but one testimony of one God.[29]

During my time as a director of the Center for Advanced Studies in Christian Ministry at the University of Glasgow in Scotland, I served on the National Board of Mission for the Church of Scotland in relation to youth culture in Urban Priority Areas (UPAs). One of our long-term foci was the

---

29. Cheryl Sanders, *Ministry at the Margins: The Prophetic Mission of Women, Youth and the Poor* (Downers Grove, IL: InterVarsity Press, 1997), 92, 98.

development of drop-in centers to provoke cultural and ethnic reconciliation within urban areas that have had an influx of asylum seekers relocating to the area from throughout Africa and Eastern Europe. In all of the UK, Glasgow had the largest per capita influx of asylum seekers—an increase of just over 6,000 families in a matter of months.

One parish that my students had been working with was in the Sighthill neighborhood of Glasgow, an urban priority area with severe economic and racial tension between the first-generation Indian/Asian and Scots populations. Within just one year, it had shifted the primary language spoken in the neighborhood from English to Farsi. Glasgow is also a city where racial and sectarian violence have been part of everyday life in many areas. And Sighthill was no exception. Our work had piloted some large-scale efforts aimed at diversity education across various sectarian barriers that included creating education for communities and schoolchildren to learn about Ramadan. We also provided language support services for single mothers through the Glasgow city mission.

But much of the work was more basic and more profound: creating a diverse and hospitable community means overcoming the mistrust of those who are "other" than what is assumed to be normative. That means creating a new "language of being" that's inclusive and hospitable. Dietrich Bonhoeffer states in *Life Together* that the Christian life is body life,[30] an embodied expression of unity through diversity expressed

---

30. "Our community with one another consists solely in what Christ has done to both of us. . . . I have community with others and I shall continue to have it only through Jesus Christ. The more genuine and the deeper our community becomes, the more will everything else between us recede, the more clearly and purely will Jesus Christ and his work become the one and only thing that is vital between us. We have one another only through Christ, but through Christ we do have one another, wholly, and for all eternity." Dietrich Bonhoeffer, *Life Together* (New York: HarperCollins, 1954), 23, 25–26.

in the dynamic unity of the Trinity and called forth in the church as the shape and substance of our witness. This meant that we had to blur the boundaries between church and culture, economy and race; and these lines had been drawn deep within the hearts and minds of many young people by generations of fear. This call to body life is ultimately the context for all ministries to youth, and it's through grace alone that this is possible and the gift of community amidst diversity is made possible through Christ.

Cultivating a welcoming and supportive environment is central for ministry to youth—and that takes hard work. When I served on the board of directors for New Horizons in Seattle—an outreach program based in inner-city Seattle that works with homeless teens—I was amazed at the basic message the caseworkers communicated over and over again: *They don't have to listen to us—we have to earn the right to be heard by these teens.* Programs and techniques are fine, but it's a theology of presence that makes the difference in the long run." It's the persistent presence of these kinds of ministries that have made a profound difference because they don't buy into seeing racial and economic reconciliation as a quick fix—it's a long obedience in the same direction.

I'll close this chapter with a comment on the current state of youth culture from an unlikely source. Nobel laureate Aleksandr Solzhenitsyn, upon winning the National Arts Club Medal of Honor for literature, made the following comments in his acceptance speech assessing the dawn of the twenty-first century:

> This [current generation is immersed in a] relentless cult of novelty, with its assertion that art need not be good or pure, just so long as it is new, newer, and newer still, conceals an

unyielding and long-sustained attempt to undermine, ridicule and uproot all moral precepts. There is no God, there is no truth, the universe is chaotic, all is relative, "the world as text," a text any postmodernist is willing to compose. How clamorous it all is, but also—how helpless.[31]

Is Solzhenitsyn correct in his assessment? Frankly, I don't share his doom and gloom concerning youth culture. There's a dynamic openness to the possibility of hope and healing inherent in the lives of today's youth—a willingness to engage deeply and honestly with other cultures, a hunger to find critical markers in order to grow into authentic men and women amidst a cultural crisis of family, an open declaration that there's more to life than living and dying, and that matters of the spirit are of core concern.

To those with a critically passionate focus on youth culture today, there should be a humble acknowledgment that we remain fixtures on the cultural horizon as leaders in the church that perhaps has something of the Pisgah view of youth culture.[32] We're like Moses looking down into a land of promise that we'll never enter, but it's a country made ready for our students by the cross of Christ. We must meet these opportunities by fostering a renewed conviction in and for the life of faith, raising up leaders who'll model an ever-deepening character, and providing numerous entry points into the grace-filled community that is the body of Christ. This should not only haunt

---

31. Aleksandr Solzhenitsyn, "The Relentless Cult of Novelty and How it Wrecked the Century," *New York Times Book Review* (February 7, 1993), 17.

32. Reference to the Pisgah view of Deuteronomy 3:27-28 where Moses is allowed to view the Promised Land but not allowed to cross the River Jordan, being told by God that his descendants will eventually enter the land: "Go up to the top of Pisgah and look west and north and south and east. Look at the land with your own eyes, since you are not going to cross this Jordan. But commission Joshua, and encourage and strengthen him, for he will lead this people across and will cause them to inherit the land that you will see."

our sense of calling to the next generation, it should enliven and ignite our resolve to marshal a new generation of students equipped with humble courage and critical insights to go into this land of promise. God is calling us again and again to listen [*shema*] to the cries of youth and to respond accordingly:

> Hear [*shema*], O Israel: The LORD our God, the LORD is one. Love the LORD your God with all your heart and with all your soul and with all your strength. These commandments that I give you today are to be on your hearts. Impress them on your children. Talk about them when you sit at home and when you walk along the road, when you lie down and when you get up. (Deuteronomy 6:4-7)

CHAPTER 3

BLURRING
FAITH

From Moral Therapeutic Deism to Sacredly Mobile Faith

The San Diego Comic-Con has arguably become one of the biggest mass media entertainment events in the world. What started out as a small gathering of comic book and science fiction aficionados has become a huge event for Hollywood to roll out new films, television shows, and print culture that's no longer merely niche. Movies such as *Batman Begins*, *The Avengers*, *X-Men*, *The Hunger Games,* and *Twilight* all found audience support at this conference that helped them become blockbusters.

Many attendees come dressed as their favorite fictional characters (this is referred to as *cosplay*) and wait for hours in long lines to hear from actors, writers, graphic novelists, directors, musicians, and other culture shapers about what motivates their imaginations, why they see the world as they do, what brings their characters hope, what courage looks like in their universe, and what humanity could become if we lived out some of the fictional ideals their characters and stories point to.

One of the actors who frequently appears at this event is

Wil Wheaton. He's best known for playing a teenager named Wesley Crusher on *Star Trek: The Next Generation* and more recently for playing Evil Wil Wheaton on the television show *The Big Bang Theory*. Wheaton has a massive social media following on Twitter, Facebook, and Tumblr; and at the end of the 2013 Comic-Con, he reflected on the ways he saw some Christians acting in the public sphere and how they were raising their young people in relation to mass culture. Every day as he entered the convention center, protesters were shouting at the attendees and waving signs that proclaimed WARNING, GOD HATERS as people dressed as Captain America, Frodo, Gandalf, Black Widow, Katniss Everdeen, and other fictional characters entered through the main doors.

On his Tumblr site, Wheaton posted the following reflection:

> These people just shout at everyone, or drone on endlessly regurgitating a script (I saw one of them reading it off an iPhone) that uses the word "love" in a way that is entirely at odds with their presentation. I ignore them, some people engage them, *lots* of people troll them, and though I find their entire presence mildly annoying, I respect their fundamental right to express themselves in public.
>
> But here's the thing that I noticed for the first time just yesterday: many of the sign holders are children between the ages of (I'd guess) 8 and 16. Some of the older kids read the script into their megaphone, while the younger ones try to shove tracts and leaflets into the hands of people who—if they take them at all— immediately throw them on the ground.
>
> These children looked miserable. They looked sad. They looked like they'd rather be anywhere else than shouting at thousands of joyful people who are celebrating things they love. I wondered if these kids liked any of the movies or characters or popular culture that was being celebrated all around them, and if they did, how it made them feel to be put into a situation by their parents where

they had to be angry at those happy people who weren't bothering anyone, and seemed to be having a pretty good time.

I feel like these kids are in a cult, and their parents are robbing them of their childhood. I feel like these people show up where large groups of us are being happy, so they can tell us that we should feel bad. I'm not entirely sure what they hope to accomplish—I've never once seen a person engage them in a thoughtful way, much less convert to their particular flavor of religion, and they don't seem to be interested in soliciting money—but whatever it is, it isn't happening.

Unless their goal is to make people mock them, ignore them, or in my case, feel sad for their children. Maybe if they're so concerned for the future of humanity, they could take the time, money, and energy they put into yelling at people and invest it in feeding and clothing people who are struggling to do that for themselves.

. . . but I can't shake the feeling that, for these people, helping people isn't the point.[33]

What is our hope for how young people should engage culture? I believe Wil Wheaton summarizes the view of many people who observe young people being drawn into extreme behaviors and wonder whether they're truly acting on their own or being overly influenced by their parents and mentors. The question of how young people relate to, discern, critique, and ultimately live within the culture is, of course, an important issue for the church. If we acknowledge that teens within youth culture are sacredly mobile, then we recognize that God claimed them long before we met them and that their development in all manners of growth—physical, spiritual, intellectual, emotional—will blur boundaries, draw from multiple sources found in the Christian tradition as well as outside of it, and be in constant motion as they're on a journey of becoming who they're called to be in and for the world. This will require

33. Wil Wheaton: http://wilwheaton.tumblr.com/post/56061933582/mostlysigns someportents-warning-god-haters.

those of us who work with teens to openly acknowledge that the categories by which they describe their sense of faith (or lack of faith) won't always fit into prepackaged categories, terms, phrases, and slogans.

Faith communities love acronyms. There are landfills full of WWJD? bracelets to prove that complex ideas distilled down to a few letters allow a certain hyperlinkedness to vast amounts of data. In many ways, acronyms are a gift . . . but they can also be a distraction because they offer a seemingly summative certainty. As discussed in chapter 2, the latest acronym to take youth workers and many church leaders by storm is MTD, or *Moralistic Therapeutic Deism*, which was launched into the world via the book *Soul Searching: The Religious and Spiritual Lives of Teenagers*. Since the book was published in 2005, a flood of reactions has arisen around this model of MTD. Churches are worried, parents are feeling guilty, and youth workers are frantically seeking new models to change this trend.

To be sure, Smith and Denton have some great data, and the wake-up call to get serious about working with youth toward a deep and abiding sense of what makes up belief should be addressed. That said, I do worry that many are adopting this MTD mantra without a critical examination of what's at stake and without evaluating whether or not the course correction proposed in *Soul Searching* is truly what we need. Might the cure be worse than the disease?

CRITIQUES OF THE LABEL "MORALISTIC THERAPEUTIC DEISM"

First and foremost, there's always a danger in any one-size-fits-all view of biblical literacy and deep faith that values rationalism over embodiment and practice. Even in Scripture the diversity of expressions and experiences of discipleship, mission, and evangelism (just to name a few) only augments the point that faith is a mysterious, multifaceted reality. For example, in order to set a standard of Christian identity based on faith, which of the litany of names in Hebrews 11 do we turn to? Abel? Enoch? Rahab? David? Sixteen people are mentioned by name, and numerous others are noted by inference. This "cloud of witnesses" is diverse in gender, race, economic status, and degree of piety. Yet all are held up as examples of faithful followers of God despite being diverse and distinct.

Identity formation in the Christian faith is ultimately grounded in what theologian James McClendon stated as "biography as theology."[34] Our identity is formed by those we surround ourselves with and who shape us. Rather that depending on merely one star in the solar system of Christian faith formation, we—including teenagers—are encouraged by virtue of the canon of Scripture to be informed and transformed by a vast constellation of people who will differ in their beliefs, approach faith in both stoic and fearful ways, and have the courage to scale mountains and the timidity to whisper a prayer in solitude. Nowhere is faith uniform, nor is it supposed to be.

Smith and Denton argue in *Soul Searching* that "all religious groups seem at risk of losing teens to nonreligious identities,"[35] which assumes there's an easily quantifiable religious identity that we can appeal to that is somehow counterpoised to so-called secular identities. Another way to speak about this is the rise of what's been called the "None" generation,[36] those who refuse to be categorically fixed to one exclusive faith tradition within Christianity—be it doctrinal or denominational—and

---

34. See James William McClendon, *Biography as Theology: How Life Stories Can Remake Today's Theology* (Portland, OR: Wipf and Stock, 2002).

35. Smith and Denton, *Soul Searching*, 88.

36. See Patricia O'Connell Killen and Mark Silk (eds.) *Religion and Public Life in the Pacific Northwest: The None Zone* (Lanham, MD: AltaMira Press, 2004).

would rather check the none-of-the-above box than a particular mainline tradition. This is not to say these "Nones" have no faith whatsoever (although for some this is the case). Rather, fixed definitions rarely—if ever—allow for the eclectic and mysterious experiences of God.

As I've taught church history over the years, one of the tenets I've used to challenge both undergraduate students as well as seminarians is this: There is more to being a Christian than Christianity. As one chronicles the challenges of the season of martyrdom leading to the rise of the church to prominence after the Edict of Milan in AD 313; the movements of the various ecumenical councils that framed the early creeds; the hundreds of years spent canonizing the Scriptures; and the various schisms that split the church into east and west, Protestant and Catholic, Reformed, Wesleyan, Anabaptist, Pentecostal, Quaker, Independent, and onwards, one can see the ways faith is always moving in and through the media of culture. The identities of people of faith are often influenced by the dynamism of change in relation to tradition.

In my own tradition (Presbyterian) you'll find radical diversity of understanding regarding what this term means, and it all depends on the context: what it means to be Presbyterian on the West Coast of the United States often looks very different from being Presbyterian in North Carolina or Florida. We share a common heritage as a denomination, but there's dynamism and different expressions of faithful practice that aren't merely allowed, but are in many ways celebrated.

To this end I have to admit being puzzled by the notion of "nonreligious" identities and deeply suspicious of what the "religious" persona backgrounding this assessment would look and feel like. As someone watches a generation of young people grabbing hold of all the consumerism that evangelicalism has to offer in order to *mark* their faith as real (shirts, hats, CDs, messenger bags, etc.) as well as using catch phrases and social behaviors valued in certain circles but foreign to others, I'm not sure I'm buying what Smith and Denton are putting on the table. They go on to state, "A number of religious teenagers propounded theological views that are, according to the standards of their own religious traditions, simply not orthodox."[37] I suggest they attend a National Youth Workers Convention and see if they can find the orthodoxy that's being romantically idealized. Here are people who work with teens and draw from the breadth and height of the Christian tradition: contemplative Celtic prayers mixed with various social networking platforms and funded by sociological and theological reflection. If they were to look into the work of Young Life or Youth for Christ or InterVarsity, they'd see deeply committed, faithful Christians listening to indie rock and hip-hop, reading graphic novels, and loving the Lord in complete conversation with the culture that surrounds them.

In his journal article "Taking Talk Seriously: Religious Discourse as Social Practice," sociologist Robert Wuthnow challenges those using quantitative methods of research (methods focused on strict data collection with prescribed categories) to treat the "talk" happening in interviews (more fluid and descriptive forms of information gathering, such as storytelling and narrative) as a unique resource for insight and depth of meaning.[38] Wuthnow traces the historical trajectory of the reputation of interview-based research through the 1960s, '70s, and '80s leading to the academic acceptance of interviews as a legitimate vehicle for doing research. Despite the general acceptance, however, Wuthnow points out that interviews are often still used as anecdotes to quantitative research or are analyzed

---

37. Smith and Denton, *Soul Searching*, 136.

38. Robert J. Wuthnow, "Taking Talk Seriously: Religious Discourse as Social Practice," *Journal for the Scientific Study of Religion* 50, no. 1 (March 1, 2011): 1–21.

quantitatively despite their qualitative nature. Another way to say this is that descriptive forms of explaining faith ("I am not sure what I believe, but I know something is happening") are only allowed if they can be tied to some prescriptive form (the ability to recite creeds, verses of Scripture, hymns, etc. that are touchstones aligned with a defined faith category).

As an alternative, Wuthnow considers how qualitative researchers might assert "that culture not be thought of as underlying beliefs and values influencing behavior, but as a toolkit of habits, skills, and styles from which people conduct strategies of action."[39] In this way Wuthnow proposes that we give greater attention to modes of expression and the assumed forms of knowing imposed by authority figures and institutions upon the narrative context that surrounds any given issue, such as how we describe what it means to have faith and grow into a deeper relationship with God. In his great book *Witness to Dispossession*, practical theologian Tom Beaudoin underscores Robert Wuthnow's call to allow for more descriptive modes of faith affirmation in our communities by stating that faith is complex and not an easily reducible thing:

> [T]heology itself is discovering with ever greater complex-ity, the particular beliefs that are "sanctioned" by religious leadership, at any particular time and place, are deeply impli-cated in "nontheological" or "nonreligious" political, social, cultural, and economic factors. The very opposition between "picking and choosing" and "accepting the whole" is itself a recent way of imaging, often for the sake of an intended control, what the "options" for belief are today—much like the opposition between fundamentalism and enlightenment, or relativism and moral foundationalism.[40]

---

39. Wuthnow, "Taking Talk Seriously," 4.
40. Tom Beaudoin, *Witness to Dispossession* (New York: Orbis, 2008), 81.

One of the most important things to instill in young people is this very basic premise: *faith* is not *certainty*.

Because religious versus irreligious identities are difficult—and possibly problematic—to view as a goal of our work with young people, it's the challenge of churches and youth ministries not to fall into the trap of fear and anxiety merely because youth can't yet articulate with certainty what they believe. As noted by sociologist Nancy Ammerman in her wonderful book *Everyday Religion: Observing Modern Religious Lives*, faith is often known through "fragments," "side plots," and "tangents" in holistic narrative more than systematically theorized, well-formed doctrines.[41] In her concluding chapter summarizing sociological research on the lived experiences of people of faith both young and old, Ammerman raises this important point: "A person may recognize moral imperatives that have a transcendent grounding without ever having a 'religious experience' or being able to articulate a set of doctrines about God."[42]

For example, consider the man born blind described in John 9. In this narrative many religious leaders (read: data-collecting researchers) repeatedly question the man about what happened to him, but he can't articulate a response that will sufficiently validate his claims in relation to the baseline that these religious professionals have established for deep and abiding faith. Referring to who Jesus is, he ultimately states, "Whether he is a sinner or not, I don't know. One thing I do know. I was blind but now I see!" (9:25). At the end of the chapter, the man falls at the feet of Jesus and worships him (v. 38). Here we see a man whom Jesus celebrates and embraces for a faith that can't be

41. Nancy Ammerman, ed., *Everyday Religion: Observing Modern Religious Lives* (New York: Oxford University Press, 2007), 226.

42. Ammerman, *Everyday Religion*, 226.

articulated. But because it's included in Scripture, we know it's a faith worthy of emulation.

Ammerman makes the following point:

> Like all stories, religious and spiritual stories are richly complex. They are not didactic lessons or moral recipes but are contingent accounts of how life proceeds from one point to another. They encompass experiences of body and spirit, as well as mind. Religious narratives may presume beliefs about how the world works that vary from the mundane and scientific to the wishful and fantastical. Some stories may mark the chapters of a life with ritual interruptions; others may be more or less explicit about how everyday dilemmas are to be resolved.[43]

Another challenge brought forth by *Soul Searching* and other responses to the NSYR data has been to place the framing and sustaining of religious faith almost exclusively on the shoulders of churches and other religious institutions. According to Smith and Denton, institutional representatives are the "agents of religious socialization,"[44] and as such they should bear the burden of righting the wrongs of MTD to a large degree. That's fine on one level: churches, Christian schools, parachurch organizations, and other Christian institutions *should* continue to seek new ways of spurring on conversations for and about faith. Yet Smith and Denton don't take into account the role that other networks play in framing faith, and, in many ways, these serve to remind us that God does indeed move in mysterious ways.

Tom Beaudoin makes the following comment in regard to this aspect of *Soul Searching*: "The authors imagine religious beliefs as starting from pure official teaching, stewarded by

---

43. Ammerman, *Everyday Religion*, 226.
44. Smith and Denton, *Soul Searching*, 28.

contemporary religious leaders, well or poorly, through official channels, such as programs of religious education."[45] To this end, one of the biggest oversights in this body of work is the profound influence that social networking has had on teenagers . . . often for the better.

Faith is a messy thing. How anyone comes to some understanding of God and what resources feed that belief is anything *but* clear, concise, or clean. When I was in high school, I had a lot of questions about what belief was supposed to be, and I thought that most things about Christianity were more in line with the Marxist critique: simply an "opiate for the masses," a fairy tale for those who are unwilling to embrace the horrors of a life without God. So I read everything I could get my hands on—from Carl Sagan's *Broca's Brain* to *The Tao Te Ching*—in my efforts to make sense of what meaning actually was. Yes, I count myself as a Christian; and yes, I situate myself within the orthodox understanding of the faith as framed in the ecumenical creeds and Scriptures canonized by the apostolic faith. But was my starting point the church? Not really. Does my church nourish and sustain me as I question and probe in search of a deeper and more abiding faith? Somewhat. Am I clear and articulate about my faith? I suppose better than some simply by virtue of my age, education, and social location. Am I anxious when I lack clarity and articulacy on some complex issues? Not at all.

Piggybacking on the last concern, there's the assertion in the MTD industry that eclectic approaches to faith development are something of an aberration—that authentic faith is to be found in resolute allegiance to a particular faith tradition without considering how God might be in conversation through other means. When Smith makes the statement that "U.S. teenagers as a whole are thus not religiously promiscuous

45. Beaudoin, *Witness to Dispossession*, 81.

faith mixers. Almost all stick with one religious faith, if any,"[46] he sees this as a good thing.

Is it a good thing?

Smith and Denton go on to state that, "based on our experience talking through these issues face-to-face with teens around the country, we estimate that no more than *2 to 3 percent* of American teens are serious spiritual seekers of the kind described above: self-directing and self-authenticating people pursuing an experimental and eclectic quest for personal spiritual meaning outside of historical religious traditions."[47]

In many ways I don't find comfort in this at all. Teens are seeking manifold resources by which to ground and yet still release a faith that's larger than institutions, larger than reason, more compelling than rote recitation of dogma, and more enlivened than an appeal to a dead past. Students I know find grace flooding through music, books, art from the sixteenth century, and even characters on television shows as ephemeral as *Glee*, as gritty as *The Wire*, as bizarre as *Lost*, and as ridiculous and ironic as *Monty Python*. This is in keeping with St. Paul's missional response to the world as he spoke to the Athenians in Acts 17. He not only sought the so-called orthodox rendering of what constitutes the faith tradition, but he also began with a tour of their museums in order to find whatever cultural artifacts seemed to resonate with meaning. As we take on board the cry of concern voiced by *Soul Searching* and other research that calls the church to a deep state of alarm for the sake of our teens, perhaps we can also temper that fear with the knowledge that faith has always been a messy thing that's difficult to articulate and drawn from a crazy and seemingly random set of sources.

---

46. Smith and Denton, *Soul Searching*, 32.
47. Smith and Denton, *Soul Searching*, 79.

CHAPTER 4

SCRIPTURE AND BLURRING FAITH

Seeing Youth as Jesus Did—A Close Reading of Scripture and Jesus' Encounters with Youth

JESUS' BLURRY VIEW OF YOUTH

Over the past 200 years, two key forms of painting that framed Western expressions of life were impressionism and pointillism. For impressionists such as Claude Monet and Pierre-Auguste Renoir, reality is seen not through the solidity of objects; instead, reality is what light causes us to see as it moves and shifts over objects. Impressionist paintings have a sense of movement, flow, a blending and blurring of clear edges in order to show that life is always in motion and never static. What's constant is the light that falls on all things—it's that which gives meaning to the images under our gaze.

In contrast to this is pointillism, where reality is rendered not in motion but in using a clearly defined technique of small discernible points of color. When collected together on the canvas, these points give the illusion of a form. If you look closely at paintings by artists such as Georges Seurat, they appear to be a collection of dots. Similarly, impressionist paintings appear to be a bleary swath of blended colors up-close. Yet, from a distance, both impressionist and pointillist paintings take on form and meaning. By painting forms that are essentially formless, these artists, though very different in their techniques, show life to be something more than mere form, and we can see anew that our lives are transcendent in ways we may not truly appreciate.

Jesus' view of humanity in the Gospels is the rendering of a master artist. Akin to the blurring of certain and essential forms that we find in the works of impressionists and pointillists, Jesus didn't define what it means to be a teenager, and perhaps this is for the best. One can only imagine the doctrinal rigidity that would arise in many churches from a series of "Thus Saith" declarations on what constitutes a teenager. Instead, Jesus taught in bold ways when speaking of youth— and always in the context of the whole people of God. There were no age-specific youth ministry programs identified in the gospel accounts. And when youth *are* singled out, they're referred to in the same category as any person needing mentorship, healing, reconciliation, nurture, and care. In short, youth are fully and completely human in the eyes of the Messiah.

This should give us a moment of pause in a culture that continually differentiates individuals and their worth by virtue of their age. To discover what it means to be a teenager in today's culture—as well as what it means to be spiritually mature—we must consult Jesus' parabolic sayings and actions in Scripture. We must also take a deeper look at the youth in our midst and the culture that forms them. And we must be honest about our own journeys into adulthood—we must remember how God met us in both expected and unexpected ways.

Jesus seems to be still and contemplative before young people—he doesn't lecture them, remind them of how bad things are in the world, reprimand them, or put them into seclusion from adults. On the contrary, Jesus blurs the line between youth and adulthood, which challenges the practice of age-specific programming that many churches hold onto as "gospel." In the gospel accounts we'll review, Jesus calls us to see youth just as they are—not merely categorize them into submission. Jesus' parabolic method of teaching about the coming kingdom of God forces us to discover what true maturity in faith means not only for youth, but also for all followers of Christ.

CERTITUDE—DISRUPTION—MYSTERY: WALTER BRUEGGEMAN AND HOW ISRAEL ENCOUNTERED GOD

Much of what frames Jesus' teaching and discipleship formation is the sacred tradition and texts he draws from in the midst of people both young and old. As noted by Old Testament scholar Walter Brueggemann throughout his *oeuvre*, but particularly in his educational mandates for the church found in *The Creative Word: Canon as a Model for Biblical Education*,[48] we hear that the formation of faithful followers of God is framed by the sacred canon through a holy people sharing and engaging a Holy God. As Brueggemann outlines in *The Creative Word*, the tripartite division of the Old Testament of Torah, Prophets, and Writings was a framework by which the people of faith were to be centered in their individ-

---

48. Walter Brueggemann, *The Creative Word: Canon as a Model for Biblical Education* (Philadelphia: Fortress Press, 1982). Brueggemann is William Marcellus McPheeters Professor of Old Testament Emeritus at Columbia Theological Seminary. He's arguably one of the world's leading interpreters of the Old Testament, and he is the author of numerous books, including important commentaries on Genesis and First and Second Samuel, as well as introductory texts that have been formative for seminarians and undergraduates, such as *An Introduction to the Old Testament: The Canon and Christian Imagination, and Reverberations of Faith: A Theological Handbook of Old Testament Themes*.

ual and collective understandings of their journey with God. As we read in Jeremiah 18:18a: "for instruction (Torah) shall not perish from the priest, nor counsel from the wise (Writings), nor the word from the prophet (Prophets)" (NRSV). This three-part call of the Hebrew Scriptures is bound together as a single—yet at times dissonant—voice to remind Israel that the God they follow and are to be transformed into a holy nation by is always on the move as if in a Divine blur of love. Brueggemann underscores as well that the canonical process by which we have received the Scriptures is also instructive and sheds light on the educational journey of Israel as she moves from a period of certitude (Torah) to a time of disruption by "new truths" (Prophets) to a time of settling down with the mundane and the mystery (Writings).

This threefold movement of Certitude—Disruption—Mystery[49] provides a foundation for how Jesus engages the sacred texts for the sake of deepening discipleship, and it also gives a context for how we see Jesus engage young people in the Gospel accounts.

In reflecting on the nature of the biblical canon, Brueggemann alerts us to the fact that *the process of canon is a main clue to education,* a process which partakes of stability and flexibility, continuity and discontinuity. By attending to this confessional act, we may avoid the hazards of rigid *fossilization* which hold to a frozen, unresponsive canon, and to a deep *relativizing* which gives up everything for a moment of relevance . . . Canon has to do with life. And in the end there can be no noncanonical life or ministry which can have any

---

49. My colleague Dr. Sara Koenig emphasized the fact for me that the Writings are both mundane and mysterious, as Brueggeman notes quite resolutely, so that we don't lose the fact that there's a positivistic knowledge found there as well as a disruption. Cf. Paul Ricoeur's work as seeing reappropriation of understanding after the appropriation and distantiation. We are brought back to a second naiveté that is constructive and not merely disruptive.

sense, meaning, joy or certainly, staying power."[50] (Brueggemann's emphasis)

This "life as canon" is grounded in the fully embodied movement of the *Shema* (Deut. 6:4-9), which is an intergenerational
journey of faith that has people sitting down, standing up, walking, and abiding in the fullness of life in the midst of and for the
sake of God. To begin, Brueggeman locates the responsibility of
learning and formation squarely on the shoulders of young people
and the larger community of faith alike to not only receive, but
also critique and reimagine the tradition of faith in our midst. Yet
the journey begins by allowing young people to ask the questions
that need to be asked; and the community of faith must be open
in mind, body, and soul to hear and respond.

"Contrary to our humanistic education and to our catechet-
ical tradition," Brueggeman states, "in the Torah of Israel it is
a child who asks and a teacher (priest, parent) who answers.
In contrast to humanistic education, this mode of education
does not assume that the child must locate a normative answer
in his or her own experience, as though immediate experience
yielded credo insights on the spot. Children are not expected
to do this in Israel because normative articulations of faith are
not individual, private conjuring."[51]

Contrary to a set of questions that young people are to
respond to, the youth themselves drive the conversation; those
mature in faith then enter into a dialogue and journey of discovery to wherever the future of faith takes them. In this model
the young and the old are journeying forward together and are
never quite certain what faith has in store for them, other than
God's providence and provision for the journey.

Brueggemann outlines "the question asked of the parent by

---

50. Brueggemann, *The Creative Word*, 6–7.
51. Brueggemann, *The Creative Word*, 17.

the child, or of the priest/teacher by the learner" within "six variant forms" as seen in the canon:[52]

- "And when your children ask you, 'What does this ceremony mean to you?' then tell them ..." (Ex. 12:26–27)
- "On that day tell your son ..." (Ex. 13:8)
- "In days to come, when your son asks you, 'What does this mean?' say to him ..." (Ex. 13:14)
- "In the future, when your son asks you, 'What is the meaning of the stipulations, decrees and laws the LORD our God has commanded you?' tell him ..." (Deut. 6:20–21)
- "In the future, when your children ask you, 'What do these stones mean?' tell them ..." (Josh. 4:6–7)
- "In the future when your descendents ask their parents, 'What do these stones mean?' tell them ..." (Josh. 4:21–22)

As Brueggemann summarizes:

The six questions and answers clearly are not objective historical reporting. Nor are they a dogmatic conclusion that is being insisted upon. They are not an exercise in literature to satisfy an aesthetic function. In part, they are aimed at worship, but clearly worship as pedagogy, the engagement of the young in the normative claims of the community. These six exchanges show the binding of the generations, the urging toward a view of reality held by the older generation as definitional for the new generation.[53]

In a similar vein Murray Milner, Jr. in *Freaks, Geeks, and Cool Kids* talked about the distinction between instrumental and expressive relationships when working with teenagers. For

52. Brueggemann, *The Creative Word*, 14–15.
53. Brueggemann, *The Creative Word*, 15.

Milner, "*instrumental relationships* are formed for some specific purpose or goal; expressive relations are those that have no specific purpose but focus on companionship."[54] We need to pay attention that the relationships we forge with our students build companionship—that we're not just building relationships so we can save souls. True ministry for the sake of the gospel is to forge relationships that will journey wherever the ministry takes us—regardless of the outcome.

Brueggemann goes on to argue that "good education, like Israel's faith, must be a tense holding together of *ethos, pathos*, and *logos*."[55] Brought together in the Torah (*ethos*), the Prophets (*pathos*), and the Writings (*logos*), the canon embodies this trifold context by which the community of faith is to know itself and walk with the world in the embrace of God:

"1. The *ethos* of our community knows that the memory of the stones is given, settled, and can be trusted. We embrace the *consensus of the Torah*. We have a *disclosure* of God's purpose for and way with his people. That disclosure is sure and undoubted among us."[56] (Brueggemann's emphasis) For many church traditions, there's a historic location in a particular tradition of the Christian faith that provides a rule of faith not only to draw upon, but continually build upon for new generations. Yet the goal is not merely to preserve the faith—as if it is something trapped in amber—but build from it in order to reach ever higher to the summits and peaks God is calling us to.

"2. The *pathos* of God leads to a giving of *new truth in uncredentialed channels*. The consensus is shattered by the *disrup-*

---

54. Murray Milner, Jr., *Freaks, Geeks, and Cool Kids: American Teenagers, Schools, and the Culture of Consumption* (New York: Routledge, 2004), 63.

55. Brueggemann, *The Creative Word*, 13.

56. Brueggemann, *The Creative Word*, 91.

tive word of the prophet. In this poetry of *pathos*, the royal definitions of reality are overcome, to end what cannot be ended, to begin what cannot be begun."[57] (Brueggemann's emphasis) In this regard we must not only ask repeatedly for new voices to come into this community, but also open areas of leadership so prophetic voices are allowed to transform us. This is particularly important to remember in relation to how we take seriously the prophetic critique that young people will enviably bring to the forms of ministry they are being asked to inherit.

"3. The *logos* of God is the sure ordering of created reality. It is an ordering which requires *wisdom to discern*—an ordering which leads to responsibility and freedom, but also to mystery and awe. The order of life is at times available to us and at times hidden from us. Wisdom is the readiness both to penetrate the mystery and to live obediently with its inscrutability."[58] (Brueggemann's emphasis)

In relation to the prophetic canon, Brueggemann reminds us that education is always in danger of having "poetic oracles from the prophets reduced to prose. It is like having great art diminished to technique or great music 'explained.' Prose is always the language of the king, of the 'managerial mentality.' If the prophet can be reduced to prose, then the *message* can be translated into a *program*. And the program, predictably, will be administered by the same people who administer everything else."[59] (Brueggemann's emphasis) He goes on to note that "prophetic poetry is a protest against every reduction of life from its rawness, from life being lived rather than merely passed through."[60] According to

---

57. Ibid.
58. Ibid.
59. Ibid., 52.
60. Brueggemann, *The Creative Word*, 53.

Brueggemann, this is exemplified in Jeremiah 1:10, which he says serves as "an epitome for the 'new truth' of these poets":

> See, I have set you this day over nations and over kingdoms,
> to pluck up and to break down,
> to destroy and to overthrow,
> to build and to plant.[61]

What the prophets challenge us educators to remember, for the sake of the church, is that we're to take Scripture seriously— not merely as a road map, but as a way of life. As Brueggemann evocatively underscores for us, "it is claimed not only that God terminates and evokes, but that the capacity and authority to do this has now been entrusted to the poet . . . the new truth violates the old truth to which we are committed. For the old truth assumed and affirmed that the world was sure."

Relating this to educators of youth, Brueggemann puts it pointedly: "The adults knew the answers in that old world. 'Old truth' upholds 'old world.' New truth threatens that old world."[62] This becomes key as we enter into the New Testament and see how Jesus furthers the call of the Old Testament in relation to the lives of teenagers. As we'll see, Jesus also acknowledges that some of the forms by which faith has been understood will shift and "blur" in the age to come, and we must be mindful that the future was never to be the past repeated by a truly new age for the kingdom of God.

GODLY PLAY AND THE BLUR OF YOUTH IN THE GOSPELS

One of the most vibrant movements in Christian education in recent decades has been the Godly Play method developed by

---

61. Ibid., 56.
62. Ibid.

Jerome Berryman. The story of Berryman's work in developing this model of Christian education is familiar to many, but some of his narrative bears repeating in order to set up the context of how revolutionary this approach to faith formation actually is. It's a helpful corrective to a view of Scripture as static and fixed, as is often implied with models of adolescent faith formation where memorization of Scripture is a primary approach over an enacted, creative, and lived experience.

Berryman did his theological training at Princeton Theological Seminary in the late 1950s after graduate study in philosophy and literature, as well as completing a J.D. degree at the Tulsa University School of Law. While observing a Montessori classroom, Berryman felt called to leave his business career and return to Christian education by studying in Bergamo, Italy, at the Center for Advanced Montessori Studies. It was during this season that two worlds came together: his deep desire to have young people encounter the stories of Christian Scripture, and his vision for a teaching model that would be Spirit-led rather than outcomes based.

While most people consider the model of Godly Play germane for young children exclusively, Berryman notes in his book *Godly Play: An Imaginative Approach to Religious Education* (in the chapter titled "An Adult at Play") that if any model of Christian education is to be robust and meaningful, then it will have formative impact for all generations of a faith community. Part of Berryman's background was in serving as a chaplain, coach, and teacher at a private high school in Culver, Indiana; and he noted that his background with teenagers formed much of his later work. Berryman also drew heavily upon the patristic writers and various ecumenical councils and canon formation in framing his thesis for the importance of Godly Play.

In reflecting on Gregory of Nyssa's meditation titled *The*

Life of Moses (AD 390), Berryman notes there are two kinds of spirituality that we continue to teach young people:

> One is dynamic and eternally on the move, like that of Gregory. The other attempts to achieve a kind of wholeness one can hang on to. Gregory's dynamic and moving spiritually has a focus on the "upward call," the blessing and creating aspect of creation. Achievement spirituality has a focus on the threat of sin and the need for salvation. The first is based on the love of creating. The second is based on the fear of falling. Both are realistic. They are joined into one spirituality when we realize that it is only by creation that we can overcome destruction.[63]

Berryman grounds his reflections on Godly Play on the assertion that what it means to be fully human is to be completely enacted in what God is doing in our midst. This takes imagination, risk, release, and relinquishment to what God puts before us. He uses the example of the Eucharist to ground and release what he means by this sense of Godly Play:

> It is about teaching the art of playing so one can come close to the Creator who comes close to us and even joins us when we are playing at any age. In the Christian tradition the central liturgical event, Holy Communion, invites us into the overlapping space of play. Many versions of this liturgy include the phrase that God is in us and that we are in God as we share the bread and wine. We cannot force the experience of God. . . . [w]e can only enter the game and play to discover such a presence. This is the kind of play I call Godly play.[64]

To illustrate how Jesus enacts this calling to "enter the game and play to discover such a presence" with young people, Berryman lifts up eight instances in the Gospels that provide some

---

63. Jerome W. Berryman, *Godly Play: An Imaginative Approach to Religious Education* (Minneapolis: Augsburg, 1991), 157.

64. Berryman, *Godly Play*, 12.

good insights into how we are to watch and listen to youth in the midst of culture.[65]

As noted by Berryman, the following eight concepts are generalized from eight instances of stories and sayings concerning Jesus and youth in the Gospels and set the stage for how we're to conceive faith formation for young people. It's important at this point to emphasize that in Scripture, distinctions of age are blurred and the community is called to nurture and grow all people—young and old—into wisdom, ability to serve, and the calling God has on their lives.

The passages we will look at in the following pages have often been read in translation and dismissed as vital texts for work with adolescents because they refer to "children." The New Testament world of first-century Palestine did not categorize young people into the demographically specific categories of ages that we have in Western twenty-first–century culture. True, some translations have rendered the Greek as "child"; but in each of the concepts Berryman addresses, it's best to think of these individuals as young people who have yet to marry and have their own children, and they are still dependent on their families for support. In this reading, the category of "adolescent" can be transposed in a dynamic reading of these passages and concepts theologically and hermeneutically.

Here are the eight concepts:

1. In our desire to inform young people as to the essentials of a life of faith—as seen in the reflections of not hearing the flute played in the marketplace and not joining the dance—

---

65. These are outlined by Berryman in "Toward a Theology of Childhood" in *The Complete Guide to Godly Play: How to Lead Godly Play Lessons* (Vol. 1) (Denver: Living the Good News, 2002), 108–142. Cf. Hans Ruedi Weber, *Jesus and the Children* (Loveland, OH: Treehaus Communications, 1994) and Judith M. Gundry-Volf's "The Least and the Greatest: Children in the New Testament," in *The Child in Christian Thought*, ed. Marcia J. Bunge (Grand Rapids, MI: Eerdmans, 2001).

Jesus underscores the fact that youth are often being invited to play the wrong game and that's why they're not connecting with what is being offered them (Matthew 11:16-19; Luke 7:31-35).

2. Jesus places a silent young person among the talking disciples to be before them without having to perform or recite anything. In this teaching Jesus shows us how that silent young person—just by being present—can teach the faithful about faith (Matthew 18:1-5; Mark 9:33-37; Luke 9:46-48).

3. Jesus reprimands the disciples for hindering children from coming to him, for Jesus wants to bestow blessing. Young people know what they need, and they know where this deep need can and will be satisfied. Parents also bring their children to find Jesus, demonstrating this blurring of lines between family and the community of faith in the young person's life (Matthew 19:13-15; Mark 10:13-16; Luke 18:15-17).

4. Preventing youth from coming to Jesus—causing youth to stumble or not be blessed—is a matter of life and death (Matthew 18:6; Mark 9:42; Luke 17:1-2).

5. To enter the kingdom of God, one needs to become like a young person (Matthew 18:3; Mark 10:15; Luke 18:17).

6. The call to a transformed and reconciled life is not only for young people, but as seen with Nicodemus, adults need to consider complete transformation in the form of a justified and sanctified rebirth and a second *naïveté* in order to embrace the totality of the kingdom of God (John 3:3-8).

7. Youth are teachers of the kingdom in that they can intuit Jesus' presence and announce the location of Jesus in the world, as seen in the exclamations of the children in the temple (Matthew 21:15-16).

8. Youth can also be in wonder at the mystery and depth of Jesus' power to heal and transform in a way many overconfident adults cannot (Matthew 11:25-26; Luke 10:21).

Take a look at these passages of Scripture grouped into these eight concepts and reflect on the way in which Jesus engages young people. What's evident is that Jesus isn't merely seeing young people as empty slates to be written upon nor trained into a tradition they're to blindly inherit. Rather Jesus demonstrated an unbelievable level of respect, honor, liberty, playfulness, and hope in comparison to ways in which many youth programs often position the lives of teenagers.

There has always been the desire to manage youth in order to help them find the abundant life. Some of this is noble and Spirit-led, I'm sure. We see the brokenness in the world, the ways in which young people are drawn into horrible and dark places due to lack of mentorship from people who love the Lord with all their hearts, soul and strength. Yet the witness of the Gospels shows an accounting of what it means to encounter and encourage young people in a way that's different from merely informing or constraining activities.

In drawing direction from these various New Testament accounts that Berryman focuses on, three basic themes are worth highlighting in our work with young people:

1. Much of Jesus' encouragement to the disciples regarding how we embrace young people is to acknowledge that perhaps leaders in faith communities don't have all the answers and at times are misdirected. As we hear in Matthew 11:16, "To what can I compare this generation? They are like children sitting in the marketplaces and calling out to others, 'We played the pipe for you, and you did not dance; we sang a dirge, and you did not mourn.'"

2. Youth reveal the importance of nonverbal communication as well as the danger of prioritizing rational modes of discourse over silence or even an inability to clearly articulate what one feels or thinks. The Gospel accounts we reviewed remind us that what it means to be human isn't merely to be rational or

articulate. One of the ministries I've had the privilege to have my students work with over the years is Young Life Capernaum. Young Life ministry began in the 1940s, and over the years there became an awareness that much of the programming was focused on a particular type of young person—there were no opportunities for those with developmental and physical distinctions that some sociocultural norms may regard as abnormal. As the ministry states on their website: "Young Life Capernaum gives young people with intellectual and developmental disabilities the chance to experience fun and adventure, to develop fulfilling friendships and to challenge their limits while building self-esteem through club, camp and other exciting activities."[66] These are young adults who don't fit the models of articulacy often seen as the standard for what constitutes a robust and generative faith given the categories and modes of discourse outlined by studies such as the NSYR. Yet they are people the Lord wants us to learn from and be fully present with. Adults tend to forget this because they rely primarily on words to communicate. Despite this, even adult faith remains fundamentally unspoken and provides the connotations for language whether we notice the unsaid in what is said or not. Speaking sometimes even hides what presence reveals and can also obscure the honesty of not knowing fully. In a tradition of the Christian faith called *apophatic* or negative theology, there's the Latin phrase *Deus absconditus atque praesens* (God is hidden yet also present). In other words, there are times when we feel far from God's presence and we don't understand—this, too, is okay.

3. The gospel accounts show the high value Jesus has in regard to bestowing blessing. In Matthew 19:15 we read

---

66. For more information on the ministry of Young Life Capernaum, be sure to consult their website at www.younglife.org/Capernaum.

that after the Lord admonished the disciples for preventing young people from coming to him, "When he had placed his hands on [the little children], he went on from there." There are no words exchanged, nor are there any didactic instructions that we know of. All we see is that allowing young people to access Jesus through whatever means they can is a good thing. Jesus desires to bless them, and it's this blessing that will remain after Jesus departs. In this regard, the young person is a placeholder of God's sustaining presence among us as one who has been claimed and sustained by the living Lord. True, they might not understand the full ramifications of what this blessing means, but we're invited to participate in this journey of discovery as one who is spending time with the Lord in faithfulness. It is in such mutual blessing between youth and adults that mature spirituality is primarily revealed.

CHAPTER 5

BLURRING
YOUTH

What the Sacredly Mobile Adolescent,
Globalization, and Social Media
Are Showing Us about the Future

This chapter seeks to introduce an understanding of contemporary adolescent development by what I've called "sacred mobility." To see youth as "sacredly mobile" is to acknowledge that in and with the hybridity of cultures that surround us—ethnicities, races, economic diversity, high and low culture—youth workers face a wonderful challenge to be in ministry to and with youth as an act of equipping them for mobility rather than fixity. This sacred mobility harkens back to the holy displacement of Israel referred to in Psalm 137. As with sacredly mobile adolescents, Israel is placed in a land where the sense of "here" has eroded to the point that what is appealed to as home is actually spoken of as a mystical "there."

With sacredly mobile adolescents, "there" is not *there*—it doesn't signify distant space as much as it marks the alienated space of a "foreign land" (v. 4). The psalmist knows his place to be *Eretz Sham*, the land of "there." The psalmist defines his "here" in terms of living on the other side, the land beyond the rivers where strangeness eclipses the familiar markers that would enable him to say "here am I." In a way, what today's youth experience in the world of fast-moving, ever-changing, blurring boundaries is the displacement and relocation of *eretz sham*—a constant state of foreignness and never quite arriving. Today's youth are always in motion, always seeking the next horizon— and they are always being led by the hand of God in ways that, at times, are found only in the still small voice amidst the storm.

FROM CULTURED TO SACREDLY MOBILE

As seen in chapter 1, some contemporary models for engaging youth culture can be a drive to get at one singular way of being a Christian in the world—always defining faith by what we're not, rather than whose we are. This model can lose sight of the inherent depth of what real life often holds in regard to faith that isn't quite finished developing. Rather than seek a one-size-fits-all model of faith formation, the canon of Scripture, as noted by Walter Brueggeman and the modes of being with young people in the New Testament accounts of Jesus highlighted in Jerome Berryman's work, challenge us to reconsider what teenagers need.

One way to think about adolescent development in the midst of a globalized culture that's saturated with social media is to draw insights from teens who have bridged multiple cultures simultaneously and see how they relate to others in our twenty-first–century culture in general. One population that provides direct insight into this bridging of accelerating cultural changes is the children of missionary parents, also called *missionary kids* (MKs), *third culture kids* or *trans-culture kids* (TCKs). A few decades ago these youth represented a minority experience for young people. But given the recent acceleration of globalization and social networking, today's teenagers by and large share most of the developmental distinctives found in this population.

As evidenced in the research on TCKs, the assumption is that youth raised by missionary parents essentially live biculturally—between the culture of their parents' families of origin and the missionary context that the MKs have developed within as children.[67] For example, as noted by researchers Clyde Austin and John Beyer, the Summer Institute of Linguistics training program, which trains thousands of missionaries from a number of sending agencies, outlined guidelines for positive adjustment of missionary youth in transitional processes. "The areas covered are self-image, trust-bond relationships, educational preparation, motivation, adjustment, and bicultural experience."[68]

While the descriptions of TCKs found in such peer-reviewed journals as *International Bulletin of Missionary Research* and *Missiology* offer some helpful insights toward dealing with the growing mobility of youth, how we speak of youth who transcend cultures needs to be expanded in the literature beyond the MK and TCK. In particular, the phrases *missionary kid* and *third culture kid* provide inappropriate theological frames for viewing how today's teenagers negotiate and move betwixt and between cultures. As will be seen in the study I co-authored (later on in this chapter), contemporary identity formation for today's teenagers in an ever-changing, ever-shifting global cultural context requires those working with youth to acknowledge that teens are anything but locked into one particular cultural context. This means churches and ministries working with teenagers need to shift how they approach faith formation for teens away from models that desire teenagers to get to some sense of certainty in their faith at the expense of searching, probing, questioning, and—even at times—doubting.

---

67. C. N. Austin and J. Beyer, "Missionary Repatriation: An Introduction to the Literature," *International Bulletin of Missionary Research*, 8 (2) (April 1984), 68–70.

68. Ibid., 68.

For years the approach to TCKs has been to help them choose a home culture and move away from the tension of being between cultural contexts. These approaches have filtered into the approaches of many churches' youth ministry programs as well. The operational definition of a TCK set forth by authors David Pollock and Ruth Van Reken in *Third Culture Kids* is:

> A Third Culture Kid (TCK) is a person who has spent a significant part of his or her developmental years outside the parents' culture. The TCK frequently builds relationships to all of the cultures, while not having full ownership in any. Although elements from each culture may be assimilated into the TCK's life experience, the sense of belonging is in relationship to others of similar background.[69]

Pollock and Van Reken argue that when a young person grows up overseas, rather than finding themselves lost between two oppositional cultures, they develop a certain set of traits that stem from growing up as acculturated subjects grounded in neither their parent culture nor their host culture, but rather a third culture. In her article "Three Generations of Third Culture Kids," Donna Wenger expressed the TCK designation in this way:

> MK—an appellation I grew up with; I was a missionary kid. And to compound the acronym burden, I was also a PK. Truth be told, however, there was nothing onerous in my childhood as a missionary kid and as a preacher's kid. In fact, growing up, I always felt a cachet of pride at being one of those exotic creatures—a missionary kid. I also experienced the suspension of being caught between two cultures, benefiting from both, belonging completely to neither. [I did learn] the term for this feeling—third culture kid—TCK.[70]

---

69. D. C. Pollock and R. E. Van Reken, *Third Culture Kids* (New York: Nicholas Brealey Publishing, 1999), 19.

70. D. F. Wenger, "Three Generations of Third Culture Kids," *Brethren in Christ History and Life* 29 (3) (2006), 256.

While the attempt set forth with the designation "third culture" provides a move away from the MK's implied binary opposition of cultures, the TCK as defined by Pollock and Van Reken is still bound and fixed in place categorically as an inhabitant of the "third culture." This problem arises in other attempts to figure and locate youth where the primary concern is imminent rather than transcendent. Another way to say this is that many studies focus only on the constantly shifting nature of cultures and don't take into account how faith may actually be strengthened as one moves between and betwixt cultures. In fact this can ultimately result not in a lack of home, but in seeing movement between fixed categories and labels as being counter to what we often call moving in the Spirit. So even the use of the term *trans-culture kid* can't correct the problems inherent in the third culture kid concept.[71] Granted, the designation "TCK" hints at this shift away from sociological paradigms as noted by Pollock and Van Reken who describe the TCK experience of "being raised in a genuinely cross-cultural world" and "being raised in a highly mobile world,"[72] yet the employment of this terminology still falls short.

This issue of constant mobility—whether in physically traveling to other cultures, gathering numerous friends via social media, or listening to music and consuming videos from other cultures—means that trying to locate teen experiences and

---

71. Ferdinand de Saussure asserts in *Cours de linguistique générale (Course in General Linguistics)* that the link between signifier and sign is ultimately arbitrary within a language system; but not all signs provide an easy, let alone correct, path to the signifier in question. Also, the signs in and of themselves will recall that which is most valued (1986, p. 67). Where the sign "MK" points to the signifier "missionary," and the signs "TCK" and "trans-culture kid" point to the primary signifier "culture," our sign "sacredly mobile" turns our attention to that which ultimately signifies purposeful and deep meaning-making: the sacred. In short, the assumption is that identity that is deep and robust is always grounded in theological rather than simply sociological dimensions of personhood.

72. Pollock and Van Reken, *Third Culture Kids*, 22.

how they ground their faith transcends traditional descriptions inferred by some ministry models. For the purposes of the study that will be reflected on throughout this chapter, we looked at the issue of mobility in culture, media, social networking, and physical location as framing events in teenagers' self-awareness. As our study demonstrates, for those who've been traditionally labeled MKs and TCKs it's not their specific experiences that unite them, but their lack of a single, definable home.

In short, to understand these youth is to embrace the fluidity of locale as normative for their identity in Christ—as denoted by the phrase "the sacredly mobile." As the study is discussed, it will become apparent that this notion of "sacred mobility" can and should be extended to how we understand teenagers in general, given the globalized and social media–connected nature of life in this century.

THE RISE OF THE SACREDLY MOBILE ADOLESCENT

We see over and over again that sacred mobility is played out as the experience of many young people for whom depth of being is moved by the initiative of God's calling regardless of cultural location. The sacredly mobile adolescent exhibits a strength in faith that comes from being constantly mobile amidst an overtly secularized culture, because neither locale nor environment is viewed as a primary source by which identity is to be formed. This notion of being sacredly mobile is in contrast to theories of adolescence throughout the twentieth century that viewed adolescent development as something to be essentially controlled and grounded primarily by culture.

G. Stanley Hall's 1904 two-volume seminal work *Adolescence: Its Psychology and Its Relations to Physiology, Anthropology, Sociology, Crime, Religion and Education* was a primary force behind the current view of youth as best served through restriction rather than expression of selfhood. For Hall, the favored student of Harvard psychology professor William James, adolescence represented "this golden stage when life glisters and crepitates . . . . It is the vernal season of the heart and the greatest stimuli for the imagination."[73] However, it's a season of the heart that needs to be restrained. Hall's concern stemmed in part from his reading of Henry Drummond's 1894 *Ascent of Man*, whereby the individual soul was a microcosm of the whole living world, an "echo chamber" within which the evolution of past generations resounded.

One natural consequence of this view was that "the current evolution of each individual had profound implications . . . for the race as a whole. Incorrect development would result in the death of a civilization."[74] As noted by David White, "Hall viewed life as holding finite life energy, and predicted that wasting it in adolescence would leave a spent adulthood. . . . [according to Hall] it was the duty of society to build 'dams' to contain and control the energies of youth."[75] Hall's restrictive concern for adolescence became "a primary rationale for various means of social control, such as that characterized in the high school movement, the YMCA, Scouting, Christian youth groups, association meetings, and the juvenile justice system."[76] Because they constantly move in and out of cultures, sacredly mobile adolescents not only have to learn new cultural

73. G. S. Hall, *Adolescence: Its Psychology and Its Relations to Physiology, Anthropology, Sociology, Crime, Religion and Education* (Vol. 2) (New York: Appleton, 1904), 450.

74. J. Savage, *Teenage: The Creation of Youth Culture: 1875-1945* (New York: Viking, 2007) [Kindle iPad version—location 1543-1544] Retrieved from Amazon.com.

75. D. F. White, "The Vocation of Youth . . . as Youth," *Insights: The Faculty Journal of Austin Seminary* 123 (2) (Spring 2008), 8.

76. D. F. White, "The Vocation of Youth . . . as Youth," 8.

rules, but also understand who they are in relationship to and, at times, despite the surrounding culture(s).

SACREDLY MOBILE ADOLESCENTS AND THE IMAGO DEI

Rather than seeking affiliation and grounding within the confines of a cultural matrix, sacredly mobile adolescents exhibit a confidence in the *Imago Dei* (Image of God) that at times defies easy labels. The notable quotation by St. Augustine in this regard is *Noli foras ire, in te ipsum redi; in interiore homine habitat veritas* ("Do not go abroad. Return within yourself. In the inward man dwells truth").[77] Augustine is in line with Plato before him in his search for a unifying principle under and throughout the oppositions and complex divisions of the world.

But Augustine sets a new direction in his use of *in interiore homine* as the *habitat veritas*. Augustine asserts that humanity, as fashioned in the *Imago Dei*, sees this *Imago Dei* primarily in searching ever deeper into the form of the self, which is the form of God. In this way, by looking to the form of being (triune yet singular) rather than the content or import of being in order to find possible affinity with God, Augustine provides what seems to be a reasonable account for the possibility of relationship between God and subject—form fits form. As Augustine states with regard to this mimesis of the Trinitarian God and the Trinitarian self:

> We both [the Divine and subject] exist, and know that we exist, and rejoice in this existence and this knowledge. In these three, when the mind knows and loves itself, there may be seen a trinity—mind, love, knowledge; not to be confounded by any

---

77. St. Augustine of Hippo, *De Vera Religion [Of True Religion]* in *Augustine: Earlier Writings*, trans. J. H. S. Burleigh (London: SCM Press, 1953), 253.

intermixture, although each exists in itself, and all mutually in all, or each in the other two, or the other two in each.[78]

Many sacredly mobile adolescents share this understanding of self first grounded in the *Imago Dei* that is *in interiore homine* before culturally fixed. No matter where they are, it's a part of them and, so, it affects how they perceive the world.

But that's incomplete because what good does it do a person if a sacredly mobile adolescent has an easier time changing cultures? If anything, it seems like it would be divisive because now you have a class of culturally transitive elite teenagers whose gifting causes them to feel more comfortable *leaving* a place than staying there. But thankfully that's not the case. If Christ calls us to serve one another, then we should serve to the fullest of our abilities, utilizing all of our strengths and all of our weaknesses. As the main universal strength of sacredly mobile adolescents, how can this sense of inner mobility be used to glorify God? By becoming bridges between constantly changing contexts with a grounding in a stable God.

This view of youth as being sacredly mobile is an optimistic interpretation of the inherent segmentation seen in the lives of today's teenagers. As such it runs counter in part to the position taken by Chap Clark in *Hurt: Inside the World of Today's Teenagers*. According to Clark, adolescent development in Western culture has become increasingly segmented. Clark focuses on "midadolescence," a stage of life in which young people lack the "ability to construct bridges between one layer and another" and are characterized by "the inability to see contradictions as contradictions and the ability to easily rationalize seemingly irreconcilable beliefs, attitudes, or values."[79] This segmentation

---

78. C. N. Cochrane, *Christianity and Classical Culture* (New York: Oxford University Press, 1957), 407.

79. C. Clark, *Hurt: Inside the World of Today's Teenagers* (Grand Rapids, MI: Baker Press, 2004), 20.

results in what he terms "the world beneath," which comes from being "cut off for far too long from the adults . . . . Adolescents have been abandoned. . . . They have, therefore, created their own world, a world that is designed to protect them from the destructive forces and wiles of the adult community."[80]

The way Clark sees adolescents lacking the ability to construct bridges between one layer of meaning and another actually points to sacredly mobile adolescents living segmented lives *as* a bridging activity. This is embodied in their relationships where they create microcultures in order to organize the world (what Pollock and Van Reken have termed *comfort zones* in relation to TCKs). For teenagers today, cultures aren't bound by nationality as they were a generation ago; instead, they can change depending on which side of the tracks you live. The rich have a culture, as do the poor; East Coasters are not West Coasters; and even the soccer team acts differently than the basketball team. Cultured identity means learning to bridge these cultural gaps on some level. But at some point the gaps become too large, and it just becomes easier not to make the effort.

Sacredly mobile adolescents are built for reconciliation, as defined in Second Corinthians 5, because they've been denied the luxury of a small worldview and are more comfortable crossing cultural gaps. For them, the signifier is the Sacred—neither themselves nor the culture. They can act as ambassadors, bridging the gap and facilitating communication. They can go where others might not, and they can help bring others with them.

EXPRESSIONS OF SACREDLY MOBILE ADOLESCENTS

In a study conducted by myself and Rob Willett, a research student, we surveyed seventy-five sacredly mobile adolescents

---

80. Ibid., 21.

currently living in the United States.[81] The forty who responded spent an average of fourteen years overseas: four on the bottom end, twenty on the top, and a median of sixteen years.[82]

---

81. Jeff Keuss and Rob Willett, "The Sacredly Mobile Adolescent: A Hermeneutic Phenomenological Study Toward Revising of the Third Culture Kid Typology for Effective Ministry Practice in a Multivalent Culture," *Journal of Youth Ministry* (Fall 2009).

82. The qualitative method chosen for this study was based on a view of human experience as hermeneutic phenomenology (see John Swinton and Harriett Mowat, *Practical Theology and Qualitative Research* (London: SCM, 2006)). As noted by John McLeod, "[a]nyone who has ever completed a piece of qualitative research knows that doing good qualitative research is not merely a matter of following a set of procedural guidelines. The principle source of knowing in qualitative inquiry is the researcher's engagement in a search for meaning and truth in relation to the topic of inquiry . . . in the end it is the capacity of the inquirer to see and understand that makes the difference" (McLeod cited in Swinton and Mowat, 2006, pp. 105–106). The use of hermeneutics and phenomenology as methodological framing for research "has emerged from a growing dissatisfaction with a realist philosophy of science based on the study of material entities with no reference to cultural or social context . . . [h]ermeneutics and phenomenology presents a significant challenge to positivism" (Swinton and Mowat, 2006, p. 109). As a qualitative study grounded in critical narrative reflection, our study of sacredly mobile adolescents revealed the primacy of how language and text exemplified what McLeod termed "an engagement in a search for meaning and truth in relation to the topic of inquiry" (McLeod quoted in Swinton and Mowat, 2006, pp. 105–106). To this end the responses necessitated the hermeneutic phenomenological method of data collection in order to provide an authentic mode to engage rich narrative reflection that seeks to be both descriptive and interpretive. Utilizing Glaser and Strauss's (1967) constant comparative method, responses to the survey were collated around recurring phrases and motivational themes. This method of constant comparative methodology relates to Max Van Manen's argument in *Researching Lived Experience: Human Science for an Action Sensitive Pedagogy* that employing a method that draws us *into* the nexus of descriptive and interpretive activity, *rather than remaining stridently removed* from the researched phenomena is vital to providing research that is for and with lived experience. In this way, our study acknowledges that the lived experiences of our respondents required both a descriptive and interpretive methodology "descriptive (phenomenological) . . . because it wants to be attentive to how things appear, it wants to let things speak for themselves; it is . . . interpretive (hermeneutic) . . . because it claims that there is no such thing as uninterpreted phenomena" (Van Manen, 1990, p. 180).

Among the data we compiled from these forty individuals spread all across the world, 82 percent mentioned service as a part of their career goals. These are people who want to help others, be it through business, medicine, social work, or education. One woman said all five of her fifth-through-eighth-grade classmates are now in medical school. Of the forty research subjects, 15 percent wanted to formally enter into the ministry, but the rest all wanted to serve God through their "secular" jobs. And 85 percent of them noted a distinct difference between their vocational calling and their career, citing their career as something that will enable them to do what they really want. When asked if their vocational calling had to do with their sacredly mobile upbringing, the answer was an overwhelming *yes*. In one respondent's words, "my trans-cultural experience has completely shaped my life, my calling, my career, my major, my dreams, my identity, my taste in women, my nomadic behavior, my humor, my compassion, who my friends are, and so much more."

Home and Identity

One of the greatest difficulties and most profound strengths that sacredly mobile adolescents share is their root in a single idea: homelessness and constant movement. Moving between physical locales, through cyberspace and social media, or between expressions of faith means that attempts to ground teenagers in one culture over and against another is increasingly difficult. Sophia M., an Australian sacredly mobile adolescent from Papua, New Guinea, wrote the following:

> Sometimes I think the cement of my being was taken from one cultural mold before it cured and forced into other molds, one after the other, retaining bits of the form of each, but producing a finished sculpture that fit into none. At other times I think of myself like the fish we caught [while we were] snorkeling

off Wewak. My basic shape camouflages itself in the colors of whatever surroundings I find myself in. I am adept at playing the appropriate roles. But do I have a color of my own apart from those I appropriate? If I cease to play any role, would I be transparent? To mix metaphors, if I peeled away the layers of the roles I adopt, would I find nothing at the center? Am I after all an onion—nothing more than the sum of my layers?[83]

A recurring theme among the respondents in our study was their desire to associate with people who have a larger worldview as well as a disregard for an essentialism of location—a willingness to move as an expression of home coupled with a sense of God's call. One respondent wrote, "I'm not sure I ever feel comfortable in my environment unless I'm around people with a big worldview who love the Lord and are genuinely interested in the lives of those around them. My location is chosen by convenience to be near my family and the people I love." Every respondent exhibited a conceptual distinction between "home" and "location." Location was where they happened to be, while home was more a sense of purpose found in active motion grounded in relationships.

Henri Nouwen writes, "Home is the center of my being where I can hear the voice that says: 'You are my Beloved, on you my favor rests.'"[84] As is central to the Christian narrative, our home and our identity should be inextricably wrapped up in God. Being denied the conventional sense of home forces sacredly mobile adolescents to examine who they are apart from their immediate community, hopefully casting their eyes to God.

One study respondent wrote:

I still fervently cling to the trinkets and memories that together comprise my idea of "home." I know the weariness that comes

---

83. Pollock and Van Reken, *Third Culture Kids*, 145.

84. H. J. M. Nouwen, *Life of the Beloved* (New York: Crossroad, 1992), 37.

from being away, because that weariness is always lurking in the shadows, waiting for the moment to whisper, "You have left home and can never go back." But the flip side of the coin is that my home is no longer a place, but rather a state. My sense of home has been forcibly removed from the physical plane of geography and buildings and has transcended into being rooted in relationships. Home is now any place where I can talk with old friends and identify and share in memories that no one around me has any reference for. This relational view of my physical home has helped me to understand Nouwen's idea of our spiritual home as being in the midst of God's blessing. It has helped me to understand the weariness that comes from being too long away from God and the sense of refreshment that comes with returning to my true home.

Sacred Mobility as True Identity

For sacredly mobile adolescents, mobility as opposed to fixity is formative in regard to their understanding of God. This ease of mobility disrupts dependence on consistency and, as evidenced by those in our study, can be developed into a dependence on the movement of the Spirit through the providence of God. The sacredly mobile adolescent shows that *things* distract us from God, and a mobile lifestyle precludes the acquisition of too much stuff. If you move enough times, you stop wondering how something would look in your home, and start wondering how it would fit in a box.

The Sacredly Mobile Adolescent and Social Media: The Tethered Self

In forming this notion of sacredly mobile adolescents as a normative way to work with today's teenagers, we evaluated the role that technology and social networks plays with both the young people we interviewed in our study, as well as those whom many of us serve in ministry. One of the key cultural shifts that many people will highlight is the ubiquity of personal computers and handheld mobile devices that frame much of our lives and keep us continually interfaced. One researcher who has been helpful in accounting for this radical technological shift in relation to the development of young people is Professor Sherry Turkle, whom I first mentioned in chapter 2. She's uniquely positioned to describe the interface of the self and technology because she has a joint doctorate in sociology and personality psychology from Harvard University, is a licensed clinical psychologist, and is deeply involved in how humans interface with robotics and computer technology.

In her article titled "Always On/Always-On-You: The Tethered Self," she describes the participatory nature of humans and technology in regard to the social networks that are not only formed, but also becoming increasingly tied and "tethered" to our holistic sense of self.[85] As Turkle states:

> We are tethered to our "always-on/always-on-us" communications devices and the people and things we reach through them: people, Web pages, voice mail, games, artificial intelligences (nonplayer game characters, interactive online "bots"). These different objects achieve a certain sameness because of the way we reach them. Animate and inanimate, they live for us through our tethering devices, always ready-to-mind and hand. The self, attached to its devices, occupies a liminal space between the physical real and its digital lives on multiple screens.

She goes on to describe how the tethered self is fully embodied and disembodied at the same time, fully present and distant, in time and out of time through the following example:

---

85. Sherry Turkle, "Always-On/Always-On-You: The Tethered Self" in *Handbook of Mobile Communication Studies*, ed. James E. Katz (Cambridge, MA: MIT Press, 2008), 121–137, http://web.mit.edu/sturkle/www/pdfsforstwebpage/ST_Always%20On.pdf.

A train station is no longer a communal space, but a space of social collection: tethered selves come together, but do not speak to each other. Each person at the station is more likely to be having an encounter with someone miles away than with the person in the next chair. Each inhabits a private media bubble. Indeed, the presence of our tethering media signal that we do not want to be disturbed by conventional sociality with physically proximate individuals."[86]

There is something sinister to this in some respects: people shunning physical contact with another human being sitting next to them in favor of interfacing with technology. But remember that much of what happens in regard to social media and this "tethered self" is that other tethered selves are also engaged and at play in the mix of relationship building. This is something to remember in the event that we are too quick to demonize social media.

I recently heard a fellow faculty member say to a student, "I can't believe you spend your time on Twitter and Facebook. Why waste your time on that?" The student (rather prophetically) replied, "Twitter is not a "that"—Twitter is a 'who.' It's about people—not about Tweets." There is much to caution teenagers about the abuse of social media and the distraction it may cause from that which is valuable. But for many adolescents who are "digital natives," it's a tethering to relationships, not merely to devices. In a highly accelerated world, the high-speed connection to other people is often a very good thing.

This was seen in the sacredly mobile adolescents in our study as well. They viewed mobility as a necessary component for a holistic life; and through social media they could maintain and even deepen relationships while "on the go," providing continuity to their lives. When they move, they learn that people there

86. Turkle, "Always-On/Always-On-You: The Tethered Self."

see the world differently, and they can share that discovery with those in their past with whom they've maintained relationships. As Paul Seaman, author and third culture kid, described it,

> We learned early that "home" was an ambiguous concept, and wherever we lived, some essential part of our lives was always someplace else. So we were always of two minds. We learned to be happy and sad at the same time. We learned to be independent and [accept] that things were out of our control. . . . We had the security and the consolations that whenever we left one place we were returning to another, already familiar one.[87]

Sacred mobility exposes one to so many different worldviews that it becomes natural to see both sides of a dispute. Sacredly mobile adolescents are thus well-equipped to serve as a bridge generation. To reconcile multiple cultures requires understanding and the ability to mediate: traits that come naturally to most sacredly mobile adolescents. An international background can also help in building relationships between communities because it's difficult to say where a sacredly mobile adolescent is from—he or she has no bias for a home community because sacredly mobile adolescents don't really have one.

But sacred mobility can become a double-edged sword. A fluid sense of home makes moving easy; but when moving is easy, staying becomes more difficult. There is a seductive thrill to reinventing yourself, to wiping the slate clean. Why deal with problems when you can just move on? Why invest in people and communities when you'll just be leaving them? There can be a dark and alluring perversion of a mobile lifestyle that exalts the act of moving to the place of a god. This calls us back to the discussion in chapter 2 of how vital it is for young people to have mentors for the journey of faith to help them discern when it is time, as we read in Ecclesiastes 3:2, "to plant" and "to uproot."

---

87. Pollock and Van Reken, *Third Culture Kids*, 60.

That being said, the sacredly mobile adolescents in our study found that the accountability of having embedded relationships with people, as well as their sense of God's leading, were maintained as they lived and moved in the ever-changing world. One of our respondents said it best when he said his trans-cultural upbringing made him "more willing to sacrifice and less willing to settle." The question isn't whether to go or stay, but whether to sacrifice or settle—a vital question presented to Christians no matter how they grew up. But living a life marked by mobility frees sacredly mobile adolescents to go and serve where they are needed without giving much thought to the "settled" life they've left behind. They're able to avoid "settling" on at least two levels. They have a sense of identity rooted in more than geographic fixity, and they don't become complacent with the norms of any one culture. These are vital points to remember whether you're working with young people in a suburban, urban, rural, or distant cultural context.

As today's young people become more and more sacredly mobile and express a willingness to experience new frontiers of cultures where they can find God in new and powerful ways, the church and youth ministry in general will need to adopt a "gather to scatter" model of training, encouragement, and commissioning, rather than a settling and staying model.

Veni, Vidi, Servi—Sacredly Mobile Adolescents and Serving as Faith

In *Ethics*, Dietrich Bonheoffer asked the question that's formative for many of our respondents in this study, "What is my place and what are the limits of my responsibility in the world?"[88] According to Bonhoeffer, it's the call of Christ that gives us our place—and therefore our responsibility—in the

---

88. D. Bonhoeffer, *Ethics* (New York: Macmillan Publishing, 1955), 254.

world. Sacredly mobile adolescents answer Bonhoeffer's question by prioritizing *vocation* over *occupation*.

Of our respondents, 82 percent mentioned service in either their vocational or occupational goals. While they were open to working with a preexisting organization, they were more interested in addressing needs that weren't being met, possibly through formal ministry, but more often through secular means. One of our respondents, a sacredly mobile adolescent who's currently seeking to go to law school, sees "working in human rights is the secular (as in nonreligious, not as in antireligious) analog to being an international missionary, so in a way I'm following in my parents' footsteps."

Another respondent commented that it has to do with her community growing up. "All of the Western adults in my life growing up had vocational callings and careers that centered on people. (They were mostly all missionaries or missionary teachers.) Their goal in life was to give people hope." The overwhelming majority of sacredly mobile adolescents already have ingrained in them a desire and a drive to help people.

In addition, 10 percent mentioned wanting to serve in creative ways. One respondent, a sacredly mobile adolescent seeking to attend medical school, sees the "scientific community worldwide [as] a very unreached group. There's definitely a need for more credible Christian intellectuals in any field." The sacredly mobile adolescents in our study tend to see gaps, and they have the desire and capability to fill them.

Taking up Bonhoeffer's challenge, sacredly mobile adolescents have a freedom to abandon themselves to a calling to be in and for the world. This means the freedom of the *individual* to be called beyond choosing a career *per se*. The respondents in our study understand career development as a deeply vocational development and believe that freedom *to* choose one's career is ultimately a freedom *for* service to and for the gospel of Jesus

Christ. For Bonhoeffer, this freedom found in one's calling is a freedom in community and is hammered out through service in real life. While one can read Bonhoeffer's call to a vocational freedom in community as geographically construed, the relational nature of Bonhoeffer's communal understanding of identity transcends geographical location in keeping with our concept of sacred mobility.[89]

Going back to Sherry Turkle's notion of the tethered self, sacredly mobile adolescents tend to readily move and flow in social media as a means of enriching communal connections and bridging the divides that separate people from one another. One way this is seen is through a call to reconciliation or what theological ethicist Cheryl Sanders has called a "ministry of reconciliation," that is, "our collective commitment to overcome the barriers that divide and alienate people from each other by the healing power of love and unity that flows from the Spirit of God." Sanders notes:

> The New Testament accounts of how Jesus ministered at the margins of his society provide a strong foundation for teaching, modeling and promoting reconciliation both in the academy and the church . . . The ministry of reconciliation is fundamental to the Christian faith. It is no accident that the Spirit chose an international, multicultural gathering of believers in Jerusalem as the setting for the Pentecost outpouring, whose testimony was that "in our own languages we hear them speaking about God's deeds of power" (Acts 2:11). Pentecost is God's remedy for disunity. *Many languages, many colors, many cultures, but one testimony of one God.*[90] (emphasis added)

---

89. This point is explored in depth by Andrew Root's recent application of Bonhoeffer's place-sharing theology to youth ministry in *Revisiting Relational Youth Ministry: From a Strategy of Influence to a Theology of Incarnation* (Downers Grove, IL: InterVarsity Press, 2007).

90. C. Sanders, *Ministry at the Margins: The Prophetic Mission of Women, Youth, and the Poor* (Downers Grove, IL: InterVarsity Press, 1997), 92, 98.

CASE STUDIES

The following case studies are representative of our data set and exemplify the complexity with which sacredly mobile adolescents are at ease within their identity formation. These represent individuals looking back upon their experiences as sacredly mobile adolescents and the ways their upbringing has been continually formative.

Jared

Jared is a physical education teacher who grew up in Indonesia. He wants to return to his home island of Papua with his wife and use sports as a medium for connection between the white (predominantly missionary) community and the local Papuans. He tells a story about the year after he graduated from high school, when he was at his Youth With A Mission Discipleship Training School handing out tracts in Japan. They spent all day trying to push these flyers on people, and they accomplished very little. When they had some free time, Jared and his friends joined in a soccer game. Afterward they were able to talk a little about their church event, and a group of the Japanese kids came. He questions using tracts at all when there is a much simpler, more natural way to build relationships with people.

He told us about his frustrations with the division between the white community, which centers around the missionary school, and the local Papuan community. The missionary school is taught by foreign teachers and is open only to foreign students. It's not that the missionary community doesn't *want* to be involved with the locals, but they find they have very little in common. Jared hopes to go back and start a program that's open to everyone in order to foster the sort of relationships that can result in a "more Christian missionary community, one not defined by exclusion, but by integration with the local community."

Papua has a very poor educational system that keeps people from breaking the poverty cycle. Because of that, there's a lot of alcoholism, crime, and general low self-esteem. Jared sees athletics as a way to give the youth a sense of self-worth so they can understand what it is to be loved and might therefore be more receptive to the gospel.

Jacinda

Jacinda is Jared's older sister. She's now living in Indonesia after spending time during her teen years in New York as well as Africa. Her husband, Matt, is an engineer working on alternative fuel systems, and they're interested in using these skills to help developing countries. Her current hope is to be a counselor and focus on issues pertaining to the local women of the country in which they serve.

Jacinda shares her brother's opinion that some missionary communities are overly segregated. "Not because they've been biased, but because they haven't consciously worked against our natural segregated tendencies." She also thinks the current generation of "old-timer" missionaries lacks proper missiological training and they might have been appointed when religious fervor was an appropriate substitute for cultural understanding. This has contributed to the idea of the missionary community as being a bastion of rest and the exclusive domain of Westerners. This is something that sacredly mobile adolescents sense right away: the tendency for some communities to be passively exclusivist—drawing together with seemingly good intentions for serving the world but ultimately becoming a closed group who's not willing to learn from the communities they're called to.

What makes this generation of young people so dynamic is their willingness to learn from and trust leadership that's not their own. There's a deep desire not merely to travel to other places and experience cultures, but truly become immersed in them and submit themselves to what God is doing in these places.

Jacinda doesn't see complete acculturation as the proper answer, though, or at least not to the point at which you totally sacrifice your American identity. "It's easier to just go to a place and be there—to lose your connection with where you came from. It's much more difficult to go someplace and retain a connection with where you came from." To be a bridge, one must retain that link to the past, even if it involves the pain of remembered loss. This is one of the truly grace-filled aspects of sacredly mobile adolescents—a humble acknowledgment of their heritage without holding on to their culture as a "my-way/right-or-wrong" posture.

What we learned from this study in this regard is also readily seen in teenagers today in many contexts: a deep hunger to connect with others and discover the grace found in other people through these relationships (whether through social media or in their extensive travels), and a willingness to be in motion in ways that truly blur the lines between distinct groups and traditions toward a bridging of truth for the sake of community in the kingdom of God.

Zach

Zach is a sacredly mobile adolescent from Thailand who graduated from college with a major in linguistics. His work with homeless youth in downtown Seattle through a ministry to street teens has fostered within him a heart for the marginalized and the forgotten. He would love to go overseas to serve there, but he currently sees his work as being with these youth in the urban center of Seattle because there is more than enough need at hand without going abroad to look for it.

His greatest priority with the youth is to help develop their sense of self-worth because everything in their upbringing has told them they are worthless. One of Zach's strengths is that he feels free to go, experience, and learn from different cultures where others might feel uncomfortable. He has an ability to see through the exterior and connect with the youth in ways that help them feel valued. While he fostered that experience as a minority teenager in Thailand, he has found that this sense of dislocation has become a gift in working with homeless teens in America. He understands the deep longing to connect, along with the freedom to move and change with the changing culture.

When asked about the role the church plays in his life and in the lives of today's teenagers, his response was that it simply isn't equipped to deal with these teens. Church people wouldn't know what to do with street youth or, by and large, many of today's young people whether they live on the streets, in the suburbs, or in rural settings. The standard "tell them about Jesus and send them off to church" would be incredibly damaging. The kids already have such a negative view of the piously arrogant person they believe to be a Christian that they don't need the reinforcement that going to church would give.

And so Zach's job is to build relationships, pay attention to what the Spirit is doing in the lives of these teens, point to what Christian love can look like, show the youth love and commitment, and foster within them a sense of personal value that might one day become something more. The fact that he has now moved into a vocation of ministry only builds on his desire to bridge people's experience and his global perspectives into a blur of movement in the Holy Spirit.

These three stories illustrate the movement and blur of identity that makes the lives of sacredly mobile adolescents continually formative into their adult vocational choices. *It's not merely a moment of conviction that marks sacredly mobile adolescents, but also a flow and movement of the Spirit that's deep and continuous throughout a life.* Be it Jared's plan to use sports to bridge the cultural gap, or Jacinda's desire to work with entire communities, or Zach's calling to bridge the gap between the church and the marginalized, they all see a gap. And like moths to the flame, they gravitate toward it. There's a definite limit to how far you can push any generalization about a group as diverse as sacredly mobile adolescents, but there's a common thread running through so many of the stories we received that demonstrates sacred mobility as a means of finding God's blessing.

As mentioned in the beginning of this chapter, the movements and choices made by the sacredly mobile adolescents described here are transferable to the larger generation of teenagers we all serve in one way or another. While some teens may never leave their inner-city residence or rural farm, all teens are culturally tied to a globalized accelerated world that's moving fast, yet constantly in touch as tethered selves—both across the planet and to the person next door. All teenagers today have resonances of the characteristics we found in those adolescents we're calling sacredly mobile. Part of this is seeing the goal of ministry with today's teenagers as a continuous, ever-moving journey that's not marked by locking them into moments of certainty but provoking risk in a life of radical faith.

Another way to say this is that our task in working with sacredly mobile adolescents is to help them live into a life of motion and discovery where things like faith, identity, culture, and family will be a bit blurry around the edges and merge with different and surprising connections as we grow. Therefore, our task in ministry to a generation of sacredly mobile adolescents is to acknowledge this blurriness of life as normal and Spirit-filled, not a problem to be solved.

Nowhere is this more evident than in the Psalms. Karl Plank makes this point in his reading of Psalm 137. As Plank reads the psalmist's longing, the opposite of "there" "may not be the spatial *poh* ('here') as much as the personally charged *hinneni* ('here am I'). As is evident throughout Hebrew Scripture, *hinneni* expresses readiness to respond, in particular to a divine summons (e.g., Gen 22:1, 31:12, 46:2; Exod 3:4; Isa 6:8)."[91] An accurate translation can render the meaning "see me" or "behold me," which involves the speaker's willingness to appear at a given place and thus communicates an openness that contrasts with the hidden defensiveness of alienation.[92]

As noted by Plank, this displacement of place is "not devoid of spatial connotation, [rather] *hinneni* conveys the convergence of self-assertion and a particular place or 'here.'"[93] Because the psalmist isn't committed to respond to his captors' demands (Ps. 137:3-4), because he isn't open to appear by these waters of Babylon so as to be claimed for an act that would unravel his fidelity, because captivity denies him the freedom to assert his identity and thus to appear in his own right—because of all these things he cannot utter "*hinneni.*" Plank goes on to note that because the psalmist cannot say "'here am I' he expresses his alienation through the language of 'there' as if to say 'Here where I am is foreign land. I live in *Eretz Sham*, the country where strangeness and oppression put me at deep distance from the roots of my identity. For me, this place can be no 'here.' It is always 'there.'"[94]

As seen in our study, sacredly mobile adolescents exemplify a new way to see and experience youth in our ever-moving, shifting, globalized, and yet hyper-connected world. To walk alongside sacredly mobile youth as we are commissioned to do in Deuteronomy 6:7 ("Impress them on your children. Talk

---

91. Karl Plank, "By the Waters of the Death Camp: An Intertexual Reading of Psalm 137," *Literature and Theology* 22 (2) (June 2008), 183.

92. Franz Rosenzweig, *The Star of Redemption*, trans. W. Hallo, (Boston: Beacon Press, 1971), 176.

93. Plank, "By the Waters of the Death Camp," 183.

94. Plank, "By the Waters of the Death Camp," 184.

about them when you sit at home and when you walk along the road, when you lie down and when you get up.") is a calling to be in motion as well. Rather than fearing change and movement, we can embrace change as normative within God's economy. Sacredly mobile adolescents have much to offer those of us who may see essentialism of locale and singularity of culture as a norm. As this study has shown, sacredly mobile adolescents are greatly blessed. No matter their occupation they'll find themselves standing in the gaps, trying to reconcile the diversity of the world, and loving every minute of it.

In this regard, there is a challenge before youth ministry educators to reconceptualize our understanding of those youth in our midst as merely Moralistic Therapeutic Deists. Thinking of these young people as sacredly mobile instead will help us challenge cultural fixity as the primary determinate of healthy and robust identity formation. We can then replace our previous view with the centrality of *Imago Dei* as the signifier to which the sign of youth should reference in both word and deed. The call for all those working with youth is to join these sacredly mobile adolescents in this *eretz sham*—this "here am I"—and seek not merely the place, but places where God seeks to find us anew.

CHAPTER 6

BLURRING
THE SELF

Biography as Theology and Augustine's
Confessions as a Road Map for Identity
Formation in a Constantly Moving Culture

verybody loves the rebel who makes good. It's the story of
operas, the grand Greek epic, spaghetti Westerns, detective
novels, and television cop dramas. There's something in all of
us that identifies with the troubled soul who gets mixed up with
the wrong crowd, makes a mess of his life, seems to be career-
ing off the tracks beyond redemption, and then miraculously
embraces his deep calling to arise as the hero. Similar stories
populate teen dramas. Whether excluded due to gender, buying
into models of power over compassion, seeking slacker employment, or getting into fistfights, the metastory is very familiar.
Where other antiheroes take the path of sulking, wallowing in
despair, or running away from anything that might challenge
them—think of Katniss Everdeen in *The Hunger Games*, James
Dean in *Rebel Without a Cause*, or Luke Skywalker in *Star Wars
IV: A New Hope*—there are those who scream into the violence,
the confusion, the dissonance, and the pain of the world with
everything in them and come out of this experience with a firm

conviction of being embraced by the fullness of God—a God they find in the highways and alleyways of even the dirtiest corners of the culture.

OUR BIOGRAPHY AS PRAYER BECOMES THEOLOGY

In what was considered a radical assertion when it was published in 1974, theologian James McClendon wrote *Biography as Theology: How Life Stories Can Remake Today's Theology*, a book that argues that theology after the World War II era became so systematically rigid and rational that people were not being affected, let alone transformed, in day-to-day life by deeply theological reflection. McClendon challenged the church to return to a "theology of life" that would teach the deep and abiding truths of the apostolic tradition and the riches of Scripture through the lives of people—how they struggled, repented, were redeemed, and sacrificed.

The prime example of a theologian who lived during the Patristic Period and exemplified theology of life for what McClendon termed "biography as theology" is St. Augustine of Hippo. Rather than taking the objectivist response of offering doctrine and creedal affirmations separate from his lived experience, Augustine published numerous sermons, essays, and most importantly his autobiography, *Confessions*, as demonstrative accounts for theological truths that are both particular to his life and evident of universal providence and grace for all.

Born in AD 354 in the city of Tagaste in North Africa, Augustine is heralded as one of the greatest rhetorical minds of not only the Christian church, but also Western culture at large. Yet as we discover in his autobiography *Confessions*, his early life didn't necessarily point to this outcome. As a teenager, young Augustine ran with the wrong crowd, broke the rules, partied heavily, and even fathered a child out of wedlock. Through the power of the Holy Spirit and a God who called to him despite his running toward the shadows, Augustine's conversion to faith and his development into a great theological mind offers a profound testimony of someone who should be framing the form of contemporary youth ministry.

This call to let your life become a theological treatise for others to read isn't necessarily new for generations formed in the parachurch ministries of Youth Specialities, Young Life, Youth for Christ, and others. What makes Augustine's account theologically distinctive is that he sees the form of our biography as a prayer to God—this makes all the difference.

Augustine's early life was fraught with brokenness, doubt, and darkness. In Book II of *Confessions*, Augustine recounts his struggles with sexual temptation as he confesses to God his struggles: "I boldly thrust out rank, luxuriant growth in various furtive love affairs" (2:1.1); "the frenzy of lust imposed its rule on me, and I wholeheartedly yielded to it" (2:2.4); "The thorn-bushes of my lust shot up higher than my head, and no hand was there to root them out" (2:3.6).

How do we offer our students a healthy way to share our dark temptations that neither seeks to deny our sin and broken-ness, nor becomes a stirring up through a gross and flagrant display of temptations akin to an episode of *Jersey Shore*? For Augustine it was to have his life narrative framed as a prayer to God. Where many of our students have been told to frame their lives therapeutically and self-referentially, like a journal entry, without concern or accountability to others, Augustine spoke not to himself but to the living God. In this way Augus-tine offered the darkness and light of his life fully and without shame, and this offers a model for how we can share our lives in a living theology that doesn't fall into the trap of an exclusively

Moralistic Therapeutic Deist model that's open to seeing teens as sacredly mobile adolescents.

THE SELF IS ALWAYS IN MOTION: GOOD NEWS FOR TEENS IN AN EVER-CHANGING WORLD

The youth we serve today are far from fixed and static—nor should they be. This is the "sacredly mobile" generation: young people who experience depth of being from the mobility in their spirits and lives as being a gift, rather than a developmental deficit to be overcome. They have the potential to be moved by the initiative of God's calling regardless of cultural location. Because they're constantly moving in and out of cultures, sacredly mobile adolescents have to not only learn new cultural rules, but also understand who they are in relationship to and, at times, *despite* the surrounding culture(s). This understanding of youth culture has its theological heritage in a deeper reading of St. Augustine's revisioning of what it means to be alive as an active rather than a passive person in the world. St. Augustine's challenge to a static view of faith will better equip us for a more deeply engaged ministry in and amidst the "movable feast" that is our youth and their culture.

It's widely argued that it was Augustine who first recognized and defined the principles of subjectivity or what it means to know yourself as a "self" deeply cultured. We're people made and formed by the world in which we live, and it's impossible to find a place that doesn't blur both the working of God and the working of the world. There's no clear line that divides the sacred and the profane, nor should we too readily attempt to forge such a line since Jesus died for the world—not one category over another. That said, to discover who we are and what it means to live in and for God can't be found only in the material world given that it's a broken creation.

So how does one find God in the complex, broken world in which we live? In *Confessions*, Augustine attempts to resolve this by moving his search for meaning inside as well as outside. As Augustine notes, the interior realm of a person is vastly more complex than the exterior of the world around us, and therefore it's a more likely space to encounter the fullness of God—there's more to the spirit, soul, and imaginative spaces than even the stars of the heavens and the sand on the seashore. In Book X of *Confessions*, Augustine described what it's like to search within one's inner life in terms of exploring deep "secret caverns." Answers to the great questions of being, such as, "Does self exist? What is self? What kind of thing is self?" are informed by the senses that utilize the material realm as the resources for authenticating our subjectivity: we touch, taste, and see the truth of life—not merely think about it. Yet the true meaning of this sensory data is known only through retrieval of memory: we have to reflect on it with others and share our insights, hopes, prayers, and longings. What's helpful about Augustine's notion is that all we need in order to find God can be found deep within us. This is a reason to hope, as it means all people have a deposit of the Divine Image of God within the vast secret caverns of the self. Sin has not destroyed this no matter how horrible our lives may be or in what context we find ourselves. The reality is that God has deposited rich ore in each and every youth we encounter, and they begin with all the resources they need to find faith.

Yet ore must be mined. The answers for how to ground youth in their true identities must be, according to Augustine, somewhere in the deep memories of our souls. Those memories need to be awakened in some way. But they can be so remote that unless these memories held within us are retrieved and reconstructed so as to be lived out in faith, they will remain hidden, quiet, and without the awakening power of God's grace. This gives theological weight to why we hang out with youth and build 24/7 relationships with them. And not merely in church, but in all areas of life so they may discover the rich ore of faith that God has placed inside of them to fuel the lives they were born to live.

The manifold ways in which we dig deeper into these secret caverns also points to the fact that rather than one individual or a singular substance or event, it's not merely the cross talk at the end of camp that matters. Augustine found the self to be complex and inwardly divided with many layers that all lead back to the presence of God that can be encountered in many ways, through many sources, through many ages of our life.

This really hit home for me when I was working in Glasgow, Scotland, as the assistant minister of the Glasgow Cathedral. For the three years that I was a minister there, my role was to organize and lead the midweek liturgical service, as well as visit members of the congregation who were sick in the hospital. Given the number of aged members of the congregation, I also did a number of funerals. And because of this, I met with family members who would tell me their stories of faith and connections to the city and to the congregation. (While it may not seem as if planning funerals for church members in their 80s and 90s connects to youth ministry, it does reflect Augustine's point about the continued growth and shifts in a person's life that continually re-evaluates how their youth framed and underscored a belief in God.)

In one instance I was meeting with a family who was planning the funeral for a former elder of the church. He was a quiet man who rarely spoke during church meetings and would sit in the same pew week after week. To be honest, until the family requested that I perform this man's funeral, I didn't know anything about him except for his name. So on a Saturday afternoon a week prior to the funeral, I met with the family in the small West End flat of the man's daughter and son-in-law. Their children were in the next room watching cartoons while I sat with the couple, eating biscuits and drinking tea in painful silence. I didn't know why they'd requested me since the senior minister had known the family for years, and I didn't know what they expected from me.

I asked the daughter a question that I thought would be rather simple: "Can you tell me something about your father that you'd like me to share at the funeral?" She turned to her husband who looked back in calm silence, and then she turned to me and simply said, "I don't know what to say. We rarely spoke. He never came to visit us after we were married, and he didn't acknowledge his grandchildren because we go to a Catholic church." It was then that I started to put the pieces together. I scanned the room and saw the St. Joseph's candle on the mantle, the certificate their son received from his Catholic school, and the Celtic Football Club jersey draped over a chair in the corner.

The story was an all-too-typical one in Glasgow where the tensions between Catholic and Protestant families were a serious matter. To marry "outside the faith," as some would say, meant that this young woman marrying a Catholic man had driven a deep wedge between father and daughter. The children in the next room missed out on having a grandfather because of faith differences. The decision meant that the past and the future had no line of connection anymore.

I said, "I'll admit that I didn't know your father well, other than seeing him every Sunday at the cathedral. So I was surprised that he asked for me to do the funeral."

"No," she said, "this isn't a surprise at all. One of his regrets as a young person was that he had a chance to go to America on a work scheme for two years and instead stayed behind to marry my mother. He told me there was a young American minister at the cathedral now, and he actually asked us to visit once, which caught us off guard. I think he always regretted not going on that adventure to America back then."

This was one of those moments where pastorally you move from feeling awkward to embraced, and you just have to accept the fact that God has something in store for this strange moment and silently pray to understand whatever the Holy Spirit has in mind. Then I risked saying a thought out loud that in hindsight was surely a prodding of the Holy Spirit. "Maybe what your father hoped for was that we would be sitting here, in your flat, having this conversation because he knew he couldn't do it. Maybe he wanted me to come to you as a younger person who's not a part of your lives to close off the brokenness and regrets of his youth so you don't have to live with them anymore. Maybe this isn't a funeral but a new beginning for your family, and that's the gift your father's giving to you."

These are moments, by the way, that once the words are out of your mouth you wonder if you just blew it, but what's said is said. What happened next shocked both her husband and me: the daughter started crying. She shook with huge sobs as she bent over and cupped her hands to her face, and her husband looked at me with an unflinching gaze that wasn't discernable as scorn or thanksgiving. She pulled herself together, grabbed some Kleenex, and then went to the other room to get her children. She brought them into the room and sat them on the carpet. We then began a three-hour conversation—no, *conversation* is too benign a word—more like a spoken-word prayer service where we remembered her father and the children's grandfather. There was laughter at how he never learned to make a decent meal. Pictures were brought out showing a young man in the prime of youth standing tall with a look of optimism. And there was talk about how their family had some rough times but truly loved each other. The children's faces glowed, and their smiles were physical manifestations of "Lord in your mercy, hear our prayers."

That next Saturday we had the funeral in the small side chapel of the cathedral. The service was very short, and I had the grandchildren read from Hebrews 12:1-3—

> Therefore, since we are surrounded by such a great cloud of witnesses, let us throw off everything that hinders and the sin that so easily entangles. And let us run with perseverance the race marked out for us, fixing our eyes on Jesus, the pioneer and perfecter of faith. For the joy set before him he endured the cross, scorning its shame, and sat down at the right hand of the throne of God. Consider him who endured such opposition from sinners, so that you will not grow weary and lose heart.

As Augustine reminds us, our faith is formed and changed through our lives in ways that we can never fully comprehend. Our youth is always with us and the scars of those times can linger even into our death. Yet God's grace can extend past our earthly lives, and our teenage lives can still be redeemed by the generations that follow. As the writer of Hebrews reminds us, we are indeed surrounded by a cloud of witnesses. But these witnesses include those who hope and pray we don't repeat the mistakes that they made in this life. Sometimes the "dark caverns of memory" need to be rewritten, and the youth we lost to fear and the neglect of love will need to be given a new face—in this case, the face of grandchildren who, when they smiled, looked a lot like their grandfather.

For Augustine, while God can be known through his created order, the Divine can never be directly known due to the fallen nature of the world. This was perplexing to Augustine. His answer: God has formed us in the *Imago Dei*—the Image of God—and those animated by the divine spark have access to the living God deep within them. This is the "deep calls to deep" of Psalm 42:7

and the location of the "gentle whisper" of 1 Kings 19:12 that can be found only when we quiet ourselves and turn inward so we may be drawn upward. This allows the soul to be the solid place in an ever-changing world. Objects in the world are merely to be seen as ephemeral in comparison to the surpassing reality of God who speaks to us through the Holy Spirit in our hearts.

In this way objects produced in youth culture—those things immediately apprehended through the senses that make no allusion to permanence, yet always reside in the world as disposable and transitory—remind us of that which is enduring beyond itself. For those working in youth ministry, popular culture is a place for us to see God all the more: the more temporally plastic and therefore disposable the cultural artifact (think of a Beatle's song, television advertisement, T-shirt with a *zeitgeist* slogan, etc.), the more it can remind us that there's something more permanent in what constitutes reality. We can thus become who we're called to be since we can see through the transient nature of things toward the enduring nature of God who's behind all that is.

Perhaps it's surprising to think a silly pop song, a viral video, a fashion trend, or a ridiculous teen comedy could help us remember that God is enduring and lasting. But this is essentially what can happen for teenagers who have adults who don't lock them away from culture, but are willing to walk alongside them into culture (Deuteronomy 6:7) and show them that which lasts as opposed to that which doesn't.

MEMORY AND PERPETUAL NOSTALGIA (OR WHY FORGETTING ISN'T ALWAYS A BAD THING)

Augustine raises an important point for youth ministry in reminding us that memory has the power to make sense of faith.

To remember is to take that which was previously known and accepted and reconstruct it anew. For memory to be brought into full awareness in a meaningful way, it must be formulated and awakened with other people. We must share what we think we know of God, our families, our friendships, and our ethical views and have people engage those memories with a stark reality check to ensure that what we lock into memory is what God indeed wishes for us to hold on to. This relates back to our discussion in chapter 5 of social media and Sherry Turkle's notion of the "tethered self" that's actively connected in myriad communities, both in real presence and virtual life, that blur together into a composite of who we are in the world.

In this way our memories (emotions, events, people who fill our hearts and minds) need to be perpetually engaged, challenged, reconstructed, and therefore "lost" in order to be owned and made real in our lives. This is something core to recovery groups such as Alcoholics Anonymous and others that always begin their gatherings with a time of recounting who their members think they are, and then allow the community and sponsors to do a reality check as to where certain memories need to be "forgotten" (or "forgiven," which is to release one's hold on the past of sin and do it as a gift to God) so memories can be remade and redeemed. It's this *in memoriam*—memory as loss—that's core to Book X of *Confessions* and constitutes the notion of nostalgia as the latent memory of the subject as a self overlaid by false images, or "false memory," that distract the self *from* itself.

Nostalgia comes from the Greek roots νόστος or *nostos* ("returning home") and άλγος or *algos* ("pain"). In other words this is pain a person feels because he or she wishes to return to his or her native land and fears never to see it again. Life for our teens is framed by the perpetual state of nostalgia, triggering instant occasions for longing and loss without sufficient means to satiate this longing. In this way nostalgia is akin to the notion of *sehnsucht* found in German Romanticism, which the Victorian poet and essayist Matthew Arnold termed a "wistful, soft, tearful longing" that's a deeper form of joy.[95] For example, fandom culture surrounding everything from sports teams to youth culture conventions (e.g., Comic-Con, *Star Trek*, *Buffy the Vampire Slayer*, *Firefly*, *Twilight*) consist of attempts to reconstruct romantic memories as present realities through communal sharing and reconstructing. Shared clothing, shared chants and songs, and shared material artifacts that ground these memories are key and yet never completely fulfilling since we can't bring back the past nor fully correct it, but only glimpse at it. Hence our need to endlessly repeat activities—another year, another convention or opportunity to see our favorite team play the same game with the same rules.

In this way youth culture is a prime place of meaning-making for the teenager, given the way it leaves youth in a state of longing for "something more." And that's all the more reason to walk the cultural highways and byways with our teens rather than shelter them. The invariable ending of the pop song, the change in fashions from one season to the next, the rapid-fire flipping of television channels creating a blur of images, and the maintaining of multiple open windows on a computer screen are all examples of this ever-changing reality that mirrors the sacredly mobile teen who is freed by God. Into this context leaders and family who love these sacredly mobile adolescents are to be agents of memory, calling teens into times of reflection

---

95. Matthew Arnold, *On the Study of Celtic Literature* (New York: Macmillan, 1907), esp. 117–118. This notion of a "wistful, soft, tearful longing" is evident throughout much of C. S. Lewis's writings. It is key to Lewis's understanding of why true, deep joy on earth is always fraught with longing, and it's what makes "joy the serious business of heaven" as it is the context within which we long for the presence of God in perpetuity.

in order to help youth become themselves in and for the agapeic love of the Trinity.[96]

What we find in Augustine's *Confessions* is ultimately much more than the journal of a soul who finds God and merely recounts the journey. Augustine shows that our lives are indeed the text through which God desires to display both the darkness and light—the deepest caverns and highest peaks—of what it means to be alive in faith. He challenges us to do so as a prayer and not merely a therapeutic exercise of self-actualization. It's a challenge to see the world as a place that is ever-changing and absurdly so in comparison to the truth and solidity of God that resides in the caverns of our deepest selves. In this truth Augustine gives us a way to walk with teens amidst rock concerts, oversized shopping malls, and frenetic text messages, as well as in the quiet of a sanctuary—for all provide places where God is alive behind the flux and change.

Finally, as Augustine states in chapter IV of book I, we're called on to be a testimony to this truth in all we do, even if we're unsure of what to say: "Yet, O my God, my life, my holy Joy, what is this that I have said? What can any man say when he speaks of thee? But woe to them that keep silence—since even those who say most are dumb."[97] There's perhaps no greater encouragement in this age of fact-checking and Google searches that puts people in the position of always waiting to get it correct before they accept something as true. Sometimes we just have to let our life speak, knowing full well that everyone who has ever uttered a word is merely "dumb" or rendered silent before the surpassing greatness of the living Word.

---

96. For an excellent reflection on Augustine's notion of the interior movable subject, see Charles Taylor, *Sources of the Self: The Making of the Modern Identity* (Cambridge, MA: Cambridge University Press, 1989), 134.

97. Saint Augustine, *Confessions*, trans. Henry Chadwick (Oxford, UK: Oxford University Press, 1998) Book I, IV, p. 5.

So sit next to those junior high students trying to make sense of their lives and finding no words to say. Walk with them through the comic book shops and admire the patterns on their longboards. Look at the bad boy who seems to be running with the wrong crowd and offering more darkness than light right now. As Augustine states in one of the most oft-quoted lines from Book I of *Confessions*, they too are restless until they find rest in God:

> Great are you, O Lord, and exceedingly worthy of praise; your power is immense, and your wisdom beyond reckoning. And so we men, who are a due part of your creation, long to praise you—we also carry our mortality about with us, carry the evidence of our sin and with it the proof that you thwart the proud. You arouse us so that praising you may bring us joy, because you have made us and drawn us to yourself, and our heart is unquiet until it rests in you.[98]

---

98. Saint Augustine, *Confessions*, trans. Henry Chadwick, (Oxford, UK: Oxford University Press, 1998) Book I, IV, p. 3.

CHAPTER 7

BLURRING
TEXTS

Direction, Release, and Integration
in Literature from Narnia to *Twilight*
to *The Hunger Games*

Beatrice Prior. Katniss Everdeen. Hermione Granger. Bella Swan. Lucy Pevensie. These young women and many others have populated many hours of conversation with my daughters and other young women. As the protagonists of *Divergent*, *The Hunger Games*, the Harry Potter series, *Twilight*, and The Chronicles of Narnia, these young women have continued to serve as role models and guides for adulthood in our culture. Whether it's watching Tris as she's forced to choose between dystopian factions in the Divergent series, learning along with Katniss in The Hunger Games trilogy what it means to be the leader of an uprising and a symbol of hope, or wrestling alongside Bella as she weighs the cost of love in choosing a life of immortality in the Twilight books, literature shapes what we aspire to become and gives voice to what we fear and what we hope for.

When we consider recorded events—even our own lives—I believe we must approach them as narrative. We must envision

127

them as a story—long or short—with a past, present, and future; we must see purpose and meaning or chance mistaking life for a series of random footprints in the sands of time. H. Richard Niebuhr illustrates this function of narrative in life stories by describing two potential histories of a healed blind man:

> A scientific case history will describe what happened to his optic nerve or to the crystalline lens, what technique the surgeon used or by what medicines a physician wrought the cure, through what stages of recovery the patient passed. An autobiography, on the other hand, may barely mention these things but it will tell what happened to a self that had lived in darkness and now saw again trees and the sunrise, children's faces and the eyes of a friend. Which of these histories can be a parable of revelation, the outer history or the story of what happened to a self?[99]

But in many respects, Western culture has forgotten the power of the narrative process. We've accepted the post-Enlightenment conception of life as linear and readily discernible and thereby have lost our ability to make deeper meaning from story. The result has been to wean a generation away from the power of narrative and contribute to the malaise of meaning that's so evident in our culture.

This movement has been particularly evident in many evangelical churches where, until recently, a larger emphasis was placed on looking for truth in the seemingly linear statements of Scripture than the more narrative and poetic biblical literature, such as the Gospels and wisdom writings.[100] Epistles that are merely rendered as propositional slogans can provide decep-

99. H. Richard Niebuhr, "The Story of Our Life," in *Why Narrative? Readings in Narrative Theology*, eds. Stanley M. Hauerwas and L. Gregory Jones (Grand Rapids, MI: Eerdmans, 1989), 29.

100. See James K. Wellmen Jr., *Evangelical vs. Liberal: The Clash of Christian Cultures in the Pacific Northwest* (New York: Oxford University Press, 2008).

tively strong walls to define our lives by in an age that prizes clarity, predictability, and expediency. Yet such poor readings of Scripture will ultimately diminish the potency of God's redemptive, sustaining grace and mercy to the size of a bumper sticker or the benign beat of a three-minute contemporary Christian pop song.

For example, without the poetic narrative imagination that grounds and sustains the biblical canon, someone could read Paul's letters without ever being confronted with the need to search for meaning, locate the proper canonical context, or humbly seek the revelation of the Holy Spirit for our reading of the text.[101] Passages such as "All who sin apart from the law will also perish apart from the law" (Rom. 2:12); "Do not deceive yourselves" (1 Cor. 3:18); "Be completely humble and gentle; be patient, bearing with one another in love" (Eph. 4:2); "Do nothing out of selfish ambition or vain conceit" (Phil. 2:3); and "Whatever you have learned or received or heard from me, or seen in me—put it into practice" (Phil. 4:9) can seem fairly straightforward and leave the reader with a view that ready-at-hand pragmatism is the central concern of Scripture. That is, the spiritual struggle isn't thought to be in the act of interpretation but in how to put into practice what's seemingly plain.

However, when revelation is understood primarily in terms of isolated propositions, we run the risk of missing the forest for the trees, or in this case, we risk missing the narrative of faith as it's played out through the storied lives of Abraham, Isaac, Jacob, David, Solomon, Jonah, and Jesus. The narrative thrust of Scripture is important because, as author Frederick Buechner points out, we're intrinsically woven into its tapestry-like plot line:

I think it is possible to say that in spite of all its extraordinary

---

101. See Walter Brueggeman, *Finally Comes the Poet: Daring Speech for Proclamation* (Minneapolis: Augsburg Fortress, 1989).

variety, the Bible is held together by a single plot. It is one that can be simply stated: God creates the world, the world gets lost; God seeks to restore the world to the glory for which he created it. That means that the Bible is a book about you and me, whom he also made and lost and continually seeks, so you might say that what holds it together more than anything else is us.[102]

In this chapter I'll discuss three critical uses of narrative in the context of faith formation. In the course of this discussion, I'll use Scripture and other narrative sources, exemplified in reflections drawn from C. S. Lewis's Chronicles of Narnia to show that fiction can and should be used to make faith accessible to teenagers who are resistant to things transcendent, people whom Friedrich Schleiermacher, the nineteenth-century theologian and father of modern theology, termed the "cultured despisers of religion."[103] More particularly, this chapter will focus on how narrative can provide direction, release, and integration in faith formation toward an articulation of our lives as things of beauty—what I will refer to as "the life poetic."

DIRECTION: NARRATIVE AS A SYLLABUS FOR THE ETERNAL QUEST

Few plot devices feature as prominently in the literary tradition as the quest. While the notion of the quest is familiar to many, thanks to epic films such as The Lord of the Rings trilogy, I wish to reclaim the term in relation to faith formation for young people in contemporary culture. In its literary tradition,

---

102. Frederick Buechner, *The Clown in the Belfry: Writings on Faith and Fiction* (New York: HarperCollins, 1992), 44.

103. See Frederich Schleiermacher, *On Religion: Speeches to Its Cultured Despisers,* trans. John Oman (New York: Harper Torchbooks, [1893] 1958).

a quest reaches back to the medieval romantic tradition as being a chivalrous enterprise usually involving an adventurous journey. True, our culture is largely a visual and sonic culture. But my desire to reimagine the theme of the quest in its literary heritage is also to ground the tradition of the quest to the ways in which youth have been apprenticed into maturity for centuries.

As has been discussed throughout this book, adolescence is a time of great mobility. This notion of sacred mobility isn't movement just for movement's sake. Because of God's presence in our lives, it's movement and mobility with purpose. This points to the ways in which the quest motif provides a means by which young people can chart their journeys against the fictive journeys they encounter in literature to give them confidence as well as caution in the choices they make in their own quests to discover God's purpose and call in their lives. This will continue into the next chapter in the discussion of a tradition of literature known as the *Bildungsroman* or coming-of-age novel, and it will also provide a way to read the cultural resources of films and mass media that young people are immersed in with a deeper and more abiding point of reference.

The theme of the quest is one that C. S. Lewis employs prominently throughout his Chronicles of Narnia series, most notably in *The Silver Chair* and *The Voyage of the "Dawn Treader."* As with most literature, especially in the fantasy genre such as *The Hunger Games*, The Harry Potter series, or *Twilight*, the text can engage the reader on multiple levels. For our purposes, there are four primary tiers of meaning for a work that utilizes a quest motif: the *literal story* level (the story is merely the story), the *analogy* level (the story is analogous to something else), the *moral* or *character* level (the story imparts a deeper meaning for how one organizes one's earthly existence), and the *anagogical* level (the story directs the reader beyond itself, beyond comparisons or analogies, and beyond the earthly concerns of the moment toward a religious or mystical transcendence and deep awakening of *sehnsucht* or joy).[104]

As we shall see in *The Silver Chair* and *The Voyage of the "Dawn Treader,"* Lewis carries the reader not only through the literal level of a quest story, but to an anagogical or transcendent level where faith formation can and often does take shape. This anagogical or transcendent level is in the tradition of one of the most formative works of literature in Western culture: Sir Thomas Malory's "The Tale of the Sangreal" from *Le Morte d'Arthur*, where the quest for the Holy Grail provides a lens for our search for meaning as one "looking through a glass darkly" to view humanity's broken nature and search for truth. As Madeleine L'Engle, author of *A Wrinkle in Time*, wrote, "there is an allegorical level to [Lewis's] stories, and, when he is at his best, an anagogical level."[105] It's through Lewis's use of the quest that the reader can engage in not just a story, but what I refer to as "the life poetic," where the truths found in the literal quest can be carried into the reader's real-world quest for ultimate meaning.

Although the characters, place, and time differ dramatically from book to book, the basic plot of a quest story remains constant on the literal level. A hero is called upon to undertake a journey or task that's vital to either the individual or the community. Others are called upon to assist the hero, and instructions are provided for the journey. As the quest progresses, obstacles occur; at times of great despair, help from outside the

---

104. For further exploration of this fourfold deep reading of texts highlighted in the thirteenth century, see Robert Sweetman, "Micah 6:8 as Spiritual Exercise in the Search for a Christian Excellence," *The Other Journal* 12 (2008), http://theotherjournal.com/2008/07/09/micah-68-as-spiritual-exercise-in-the-search-for-a-christian-excellence/.

105. Madeleine L'Engle, Foreword in *Companion to Narnia*, ed. Paul F. Ford (New York: Collier, 1986), xiii.

traveling party, usually of a supernatural kind, appears. And then at last, there is some form of goal attainment.[106]

In both *The Voyage of the "Dawn Treader"* and *The Silver Chair*, Lewis sticks to this formula. In *The Silver Chair*, Eustace and Jill are called from outside of their world to go to Narnia for the purpose of a quest:

> "Please, what task, Sir?" said Jill.
>
> "The task for which I called you and him here out of your own world. [. . .] You would not have been called to me unless I had been calling to you," said the Lion. [. . .] "And now hear your task. [. . .] I lay on you this command, that you seek this lost prince until either you have found him and brought him to his father's house, or else died in the attempt, or else gone back to your own world."[107]

In *The Voyage of the "Dawn Treader,"* the children (Lucy, Edmund, and Eustace) are brought into Narnia to join an in-progress quest that is led by King Caspian who tells the children the task before them:

> "On my coronation day, with Aslan's approval, I swore an oath that, if once I established peace in Narnia, I would sail east myself for a year and a day to find my father's friends or to learn of their deaths and avenge them if I could."[108]

In both cases, the travelers are given instructions to guide them on their quests. In *The Voyage of the "Dawn Treader,"* the travelers are to sail east for a year and a day through the Eastern Seas beyond the Lone Islands.[109] In *The Silver Chair*, Aslan gives instructions in the form of signs: "'I will tell you, Child,'"

---

106. An excellent review of the place of the quest in comparative literature is Joseph Campbell, *The Hero with a Thousand Faces*, Bollingen Series 3rd edition (New York: New World Library, 2008).

107. C. S. Lewis, *The Silver Chair* (New York: Macmillan, 1952), 18–19.

108. C. S. Lewis, *The Voyage of the "Dawn Treader"* (New York: Macmillan, 1952), 16.

109. Ibid., 15.

said the Lion. "'These are the Signs by which I will guide you in your quest. [. . .] Remember the Signs and believe the Signs. Nothing else matters.'"[110]

As is basic to a quest story, the travelers in both *The Voyage of the "Dawn Treader"* and *The Silver Chair* encounter numerous distractions and obstacles in pursuit of their goal. While throughout *The Voyage of the "Dawn Treader"* the travelers are distracted from the goal by physical obstacles, such as the capture on the island governed by Gumpas and the transformation of Eustace into a dragon, the travelers in *The Silver Chair* deal with mental and spiritual distractions from the signs given to them by Aslan. This is demonstrated when the green Witch is interrogating the travelers as to the true identity of Aslan and the Sun:

> The Witch shook her head. "I see," she said, "that we should do no better with your *lion*, as you call it, than we did with your *sun*. You have seen lamps, and so you imagined a bigger and better lamp and called it the *sun*. You've seen cats, and now you want a bigger and better cat, and it's to be called a *lion*. [. . .] Come, all of you. Put away these childish tricks. I have work for you all in the real world. There is no Narnia, no Overworld, no sky, no sun, no Aslan."[111]

A common element of a quest story is help arriving from outside the main group and usually of a supernatural variety. This help often enters the tale when the hero doesn't expect it and when it's most needed. In *The Voyage of the "Dawn Treader,"* this is displayed when Eustace becomes a dragon: "He had turned into a dragon while he was asleep. Sleeping on a dragon's hoard with greedy, dragonish thoughts in his heart, he had become a dragon himself." At the moment of Eustace's greatest despair, Aslan arrives to help: "I was lying awake and

---

110. Lewis, *The Silver Chair*, 19, 21.
111. Lewis, *The Silver Chair*, 157.

wondering what on earth would become of me. And then [. . .]
I looked up and saw the very last thing I expected: a huge lion
coming slowly toward me."[112]

The attainment of the goal is just as essential to a quest
story as any other element. Yet, often a secondary goal attainment will occur during the journey that wasn't planned by the
travelers and it's often this unplanned goal that gives the quest
its transcendent purpose. In *The Voyage of the "Dawn Treader,"*
the seemingly primary goal of discovering the whereabouts of
the seven lords is attained, and the crew of the *Dawn Treader*
"all reached Narnia in the end." A secondary goal attainment
was that of Eustace's redemption as a result of his journey to
Narnia: "back in our own world everyone soon started saying
how Eustace had improved, and how 'You'd never know him
for the same boy.'"[113]

Apart from its strength as a literary device, the theme of the
quest provides a powerful *anagogical or transcendent* medium
for the reader to engage in as well. The story can capture the
reader with the plot and action of the story, while also impart-
ing higher ideals that the reader can integrate personally into
the real world. An example of this is vividly displayed in Sir
Thomas Malory's *Le Morte d'Arthur*, perhaps the most famous
of quest tales. In "The Tale of the Sangreal," Sir Gawaine, the
purest knight of the Round Table, puts out the call to the quest
for the Holy Grail: "Therefore I make this vow: to set off in
search of the Holy Grail tomorrow and not to return for at least
a year and a day without seeing it more clearly, but to accept
it as in accordance with God's will if this is not vouchsafed
me."[114] Note here the similarities between Sir Gawain's call to

---

112. Lewis, *The Voyage of the "Dawn Treader,"* 75, 87, 88.

113. Ibid., 216.

114. Thomas Malory, *Le Morte d'Arthur*, ed. Keith Baines (New York: Bramhall,
1988), 365.

the quest and King Caspian's call in *The Voyage of the "Dawn Treader,"* where the king states, "I would sail east myself for a year and a day to find my father's friends."[115]

In "The Tale of the Sangreal," the Holy Grail represents a search for healing and ultimate wholeness through king and country, which were intertwined. As the various Grail knights come in contact with the Holy Grail, they are healed of both physical and spiritual ailment. Sir Lancelot has a vision of a wounded knight calling him to healing:

> "Sweet Jesu, when shall I see the Holy Grail and be cured? Surely, lying on this litter, I have suffered for long, for a trespass which was not great." [. . . A] silver table bearing the Holy Grail appeared before the knight. Sir Lancelot recognized the Grail, having seen it before in King Pelles' castle. The wounded knight lifted both hands and spoke again: "Sweet Lord, I pray you that as you are present in this Holy Vessel, so will you cure me of my malady!" So saying, he knelt before the Holy Grail and kissed it, and thereupon was cured.[116]

The healing of Eustace Scrubb, both physically as a dragon and mentally as a boy (who Lewis suggests almost deserved such a pitiful surname given what a mess he was at the beginning of the tale), represents a similar image to the healing offered by the wounded knight in "The Tale of the Sangreal." After his physical transformation into a dragon, Eustace can't free himself—the task of release is greater than he is able to accomplish. After multiple failures at cleansing himself of his dragon nature, Eustace listens to Aslan:

> "Then the lion said—but I don't know if it spoke—'You will have to let me undress you.' I was afraid of his claws, I can tell you, but I was pretty nearly desperate now. So I just lay

115. Lewis, *The Voyage of the "Dawn Treader,"* 16.
116. Malory, *Le Morte d'Arthur*, 376.

flat down on my back to let him do it. The very first tear he made was so deep that I thought it had gone right into my heart. [. . .] The only thing that made me able to bear it was just the pleasure of feeling the stuff peel off. [. . .] I found that all the pain had gone from my arm. And then I saw why. I'd turned into a boy again."[117]

In both accounts, the healing vision of Sir Lancelot to partake of the Grail and the de-dragoning of Eustace under the claws of Aslan, the true quest speaks not only at the literal level but also at the anagogical level—contact with the Holy is the key to healing and wholeness.

The anagogical levels of *The Voyage of the "Dawn Treader"* are evident from the beginning when King Caspian is explaining the quest to the children:

> "Reepicheep here has an even higher hope." Everyone's eyes turned to the Mouse.
>
> "As high as my spirit," it said. [. . .] "Why should we not come to the very eastern end of the world? And what might we find there? I expect to find Aslan's own country."[118]

Reepicheep's high hope of finding Aslan's country represents just one example of how the literal level of adventure in *The Voyage of the "Dawn Treader"* and *The Silver Chair* transports readers to an anagogical experience.

Lewis's fiction also becomes valuable when set against the life of the reader. Aslan's healing of Eustace, the admonition of Jill to "Remember the signs!" and the resurrection of Caspian at the end of *The Silver Chair* are images readers can retrieve and revive through their day-to-day lives. The story then moves from the pages and literally *moves* readers to grasp that possibilities held in narrative can be embodied in our lives. This is what is meant by

---

117. Lewis, *The Voyage of the "Dawn Treader,"* 90–91.
118. Lewis, *The Voyage of the "Dawn Treader,"* 16.

a "living myth" as stated by Marjorie Evelyn Wright in regard to
the Narnia books in her research on the role of mythopoetic cos-
mology in C. S. Lewis, Charles Williams, and J. R. R. Tolkien:
"These stories [the Narnia Chronicles] satisfy the requirements
for the "living myth": They have correspondence with Man's
condition in the modern world, yet serve all times and all condi-
tions in that they are set in eternal mobility."[119]

The theme of the quest is a powerful motif due to its relation to the human drama. As the historian and biographer
Frances Gies writes, the quest has been developed by artists
through the centuries: "Other poets took up the Arthurian
theme. . . . painted a vivid picture of King Arthur's court and
the Round Table and further developed the theme of the Grail,
building his story on the knight's search, beyond adventure,
human love, and even the brotherly spirit of the Round Table,
for the meaning of life."[120]

In turning to Scripture, narrative examples of the quest
abound. The narrative of Abraham being called by God: What
does it look and feel like not to know exactly where God is
leading me? The narrative of Job's friends trying to tempt him
to turn his back on God: What does it look and feel like to be
led astray during my personal quest? The narrative of Jonah:
What does it look and feel like to abandon my quest set forth
by God? The narrative of David and Goliath: What is it like to
trust God in the face of overwhelming odds? The narrative of
Gideon circling the walled city: What does it feel like to have

---

119. Marjorie Evelyn Wright, *The Cosmic Kingdom of Myth: A Study in the Myth-
Philosophy of Charles Williams, C. S. Lewis, J. R. R. Tolkien*, Ph.D. disserta-
tion (University of Illinois at Urbana-Champaign, no. 0090, 1960), 65.

120. Frances Gies, *The Knight in History* (New York: Harper and Row, 1984),
76. In particular, Gies is referring to the work of minnesinger Wolfram von
Eschenbach and the various depictions of the Grail quest through centuries
upon centuries of reimaging the quest in song, poetry, and painting as the
context for providing a map for life's search.

God call you on a quest that seems irrational? The parable of the prodigal son: What will it be like to return to my quest after searching for meaning apart from God?

As stated by the philosopher Alasdair MacIntyre, the quest is conclusively more than a literary device—it's life itself:

> The unity of human life is the unity of a narrative quest. Quests sometimes fail, are frustrated, abandoned, or dissipated into distractions; and human lives may in all these ways also fail. But the only criteria for success or failure in a human life as a whole are the criteria of success or failure in a narrated or to-be-narrated quest. [. . .] It is in the course of the quest and only through encountering and coping with the various particular harms, dangers, temptation, and distractions which provide any quest with its episodes and incidents that the goal of the quest is finally to be understood.[121]

In this way, MacIntyre reminds us that human life is framed by unity and not discord. To bring this point home in relation to the overall theme of this book, we're unified to be sure, but it's a narrative unity—or a unity in motion—that will seem like a blur to those who wish it to remain static. What seems random, haphazard, or blurry is instead the effect of plotting the meaning and context of our lives on too limited a canvas. For our lives to move toward that for which we're created, we need to embrace the reality of fiction in our existence—the reality that much of what's enduring requires an imaginative leap as much as a critical and reasoned reflection.

This was brought home to me in vivid ways one summer when I served as a leader for a Young Life camp in Canada called Malibu Club. Malibu is an amazing place that seems to

121. Alasdair MacIntyre, "The Virtues, the Unity of a Human Life, and the Concept of a Tradition" in *Why Narrative? Readings in Narrative Theology*, eds. Stanley Hauerwas and L. Gregory Jones (Grand Rapids, MI: Eerdmans, 1989), 104.

have descended from the heavens as the ideal summer camp. Situated on the Princess Louisa Inlet of British Columbia, Malibu has been a fantastic place for teenagers to come and engage meaningful conversations about their lives with dedicated adult mentors who work, play, weep, and pray alongside these young people not only during a week of camp, but also journey with them into their lives back home at school and in their families.

One teen I got to know at Malibu—I'll call him Jeremy—came from a pretty broken family. Jeremy's father had left him, Jeremy's mother and two sisters when Jeremy was in first grade. Jeremy hadn't heard from him in years. Given his height and athletic ability, Jeremy was encouraged early on to get involved in basketball. Various coaches over the years gave him confidence in his athletic skills, and as a sophomore in high school, he was pegged for great things. However, he was also an angry young man who never wanted to take discussions about faith seriously and would interject sarcastic remarks whenever our small group gathered in the cabin each night for the evening discussion.

One day toward the end of camp, I was with Jeremy on the outer dock. I asked him what he liked about school other than basketball. We were watching the boaters swirling around in the water, which made for gentle rings within rings of glistening gold to lap against the dock. I suppose it was this stillness that gave Jeremy space to open up. "I like my English Lit class," he said, "because it's the one class where it isn't about the answers, which always stresses me out." I asked him to give me an example. "You know *The Great Gatsby*? Well, I love the fact that even though you know that Jay Gatsby is fake pretty much from the start, no one is telling you that. It just happens as you read it. Math, history, science all *tell* you that things have to be a certain way, but books like *The Great Gatsby show* you the way." What this conversation opened up for Jeremy later was that he was approaching the questions of faith like a problem to be solved rather than a story to be lived. As we talked more and as he began to read the Gospels like he read literature—more as a quest to journey on rather than answers to catalog—his heart began to soften to who Jesus was.

However, this process took time and didn't all happen during one week of camp. It took a while for Jeremy to allow himself to walk into the story of faith, and, as he said about *The Great Gatsby*, to let Jesus *show the way* as opposed to thinking faith was all about *things having to be a certain way*. But what this slow progress demonstrated was that Jeremy is like many teenagers who are looking for a story by which to map their quest for meaning. The resources they're finding in literature are giving them directions which can—and should—be encouraged in relation to the complex journey of faith they're on.

RELEASE: NARRATIVE AS THE CANVAS TO STEWARD PERSONAL AND COLLECTIVE PAIN

Turning from the role that narrative plays in providing a direction for the life quest, we see that narrative is also capable of moving us from suffering to acceptance of the potential healing and redemption that's found on the quest. In Fyodor Dostoevsky's short story "Notes from the Underground," the protagonist states that the only true proof of our existence is through our pain. He argues that whereas everything else in life can be argued to be an illusion, no one would purposefully choose pain—it possesses a self-identity apart from our id impulse to pleasure and is hence a verifiable reality. And C. S. Lewis argued that pain is God's "megaphone to rouse a deaf world."[122] He sees pain as God's means of grabbing our attention and showing us how much we need him.

---

122. C. S. Lewis, *The Problem of Pain* (New York: Macmillan, 1938), 45.

The use of narrative in relation to the processing of pain is multipurposeful. First, narrative provides a means of organizing the internal chaos that results from childhood. For instance, the child psychologist Bruno Bettelheim made the following observation:

> The child is subject to desperate feelings of loneliness and isolation, and he often experiences mortal anxiety. More often than not, he is unable to express these feelings in words, or he can do so only by indirection: fear of the dark, of some animal, anxiety about his body. Since it creates discomfort in a parent to recognize these emotions in his child, the parent tends to overlook them, or he belittles these spoken fears.
>
> The fairy tale, by contrast, takes these existential anxieties and dilemmas very seriously and addresses itself directly to them: the need to be loved and the fear that one is thought worthless; the love of life, and the fear of death. Further, the fairy tale offers solutions in ways that the child can grasp on his level of understanding. [. . .] As he listens to the fairy tale, the child gets ideas about how he may create order out of the chaos which is his inner life.[123]

It's through narrative—in this case fairy tales—that children learn how to engage themselves and understand social structures and reality. When deprived of the right kinds of narrative, children will not fully assimilate salient developmental questions such as "Who am I?" "Where do I come from?" "How did the world come into being?" and "What is the purpose of life?" Without such questions being asked early on, a child's world will remain, on many levels, an unresolved chaos of mystery and pain.

One of the potent ways fantasy literature does this in the lives of teenagers is in the ways that protagonists discover they

---

123. Bruno Bettelheim, *The Uses of Enchantment: The Meaning and Importance of Fairy Tales* (New York: Penguin Books, 1991), 74–75.

were born for more than a mundane life. Consider the moment when Hagrid tells Harry Potter that he's not merely a sad orphan but actually a wizard from a magical family, and his legacy lies within a grand world of wonder that he previously hadn't known about. Or how about the moment in Orson Scott Card's sci-fi novel *Ender's Game* when Ender Wiggin, who is considered a nobody due to his birth as a third child, is soon discovered to be the hope of all humanity. Or the moment when Katniss Everdeen in *The Hunger Games* defies all odds as the underdog tribute from District 12 of Panem to become the victor of the Hunger Games and show that she, and perhaps the reader as well, can live a life where "the odds are always in your favor." Many young adult fantasy novels provide an imaginative framework by which to see and experience life as greater than our current situation may allow us to see. This also allows us to discover the courage to overcome the pain of loss, just as these protagonists have done.

The use of narrative provides a template for organizing pain in a way that can be constructively expressed and therefore released. Therapists utilize open-ended questions as a means of drawing people out of their pain and teaching them how to express what's going on internally. Statements such as, "Tell me about your first childhood memories," "Tell me about your relationship with your father," and "Tell me about dinnertime with your family" are representative of this notion. In this "tell me" framework, adults can create a safe environment, like an internal cinema, where children can watch the events and circumstances of their pain unfold before them as both player and spectator.

Pain is a human constant, yet what we do with the pain in our lives varies greatly. For many people it's an almost intolerable burden. In Ray Bradbury's classic novel *Something Wicked This Way Comes*, Mr. Halloway makes the following observation to his young son Will, illustrating the burden of pain and the potential for sin that all people endure:

> Sometimes the man who looks happiest in town [. . .] is the one carrying the biggest load of sin. There are smiles and smiles; learn to tell the dark variety from the light [. . .] and men do love sin, Will, oh how they love it, never doubt, in all shapes, sizes, colors, and smells [. . .] For being good is a fearful occupation; men strain at it and sometimes break in two.[124]

Frederick Buechner expresses this idea in relation to the parable of the talents in Matthew 25:14-30:

> To bury your life is to stop growing [. . .] the buried pain in particular and all the other things we tend to bury along with pain, including joy, which tends to get buried too when we start burying things, that the buried life is itself darkness and wailing and gnashing of teeth and the one who casts us into it is no one other than ourselves.[125]

To release our pain and suffering for the sake of others is what Buechner sees as being a good "steward of your pain"— investing not only our joys and gifts with others, but fully investing all of ourselves into the life of the kingdom of God as a testimony of God's providence. This is what it is to tell the story of our life as we sojourn with others: we're to lean on each other and bandage our wounds through the sharing of our personal and collective scars. It's to be real as the Velveteen Rabbit was with all its fur rubbed off and two buttons missing. It's to be cut to the heart with the claw of the great lion, who, as Lewis suggests, is "good", but not "safe."[126]

---

124. Ray Bradbury, *Something Wicked This Way Comes* (New York: Avon Books, 1962, 1997), 135. Italics from the original.

125. Buechner, *The Clown in the Belfry*, 99.

126. C. S. Lewis, *The Lion, the Witch and the Wardrobe* (New York: Macmillan, 1950), 76.

This is an important point to underscore in our work with young people: the wild, untamed nature of God who comes and goes as he pleases. But though God is unpredictable, he's good. So often we sell young people the view that faith will give them certainty in an ever-changing world. What we see in the biblical narrative and in the lives of those who follow the untamed God is this: God is in motion while much of the world is stuck in brokenness and sin. This is the notion of blur found in the life of faith: God moves faster and more profoundly than the accelerated culture in which we live. It's the constant movement of love and life that is the divine dance of the Trinity, and it is the constant *koinonia* of the church's love for its neighbors that sees faith as love in action and not merely a fixed and static statement.

INTEGRATION: NARRATIVE AS THE INTERSECTION OF INTERNAL AND EXTERNAL HISTORIES

Where reflecting on the narrative shape of our lives provides both a direction for our quests and a means of release from the pain that's a part of our journeys, the life poetic is also a commitment to seeing the intersection of our narrated life with the stories of those who've gone before us, those who share this season of time with us, and those who will inherit our stories in future generations. In chapter 6, I discussed biography as theology. In this way, I argue that history when read through biography also takes on the depth of theology. And although history at its base is the rendering of facts and events, narrative serves as the frame within which history is displayed, revealing the fullness of our stories as they intersect with the fullness of history's larger story. This is what the theologian David F. Ford calls providing a "middle distance perspective":

The middle distance is that focus which best does justice to the ordinary social world of people in interaction. It portrays them acting, talking, suffering, thinking, and involved in institutions, societies, and networks of relationships over time [. . . and] helps to translate one mode of experience into another.[127]

Without a deep and imaginative orientation to the past and ultimate future, it's impossible to fully embody our lives in the present. As we're reminded by Saint Paul in 1 Corinthians 13, the three grand Christian virtues are faith, hope, and love: the past is apprehended through reflection upon our faith and those who have lived lives of faith before us,[128] and our future is anticipated with a repose of hope that creates the context of the present for us to love and be loved. In this way, if we're without faith and hope (or disconnected from our past and future), we can't love (in the present). In the middle distance view, we live in the present as a part of history, tethered between constantly remembering the past of our faith and the coming promise of our future. This view is accomplished through the *story* of history, which is our past framed in smiles, tears, jeers, stumbles, and leaps. As put by H. Richard Niebuhr:

It may be said that to speak of history in this fashion is to try to think with poets rather than with scientists. That is what we mean, for poets think of persons, purposes, and destinies.

---

127. David F. Ford, "System, Story, Performance: A Proposal about the Role of Narrative in Christian Systematic Theology" in *Why Narrative? Readings in Narrative Theology*, eds. Stanley Hauerwas and L. Gregory Jones (Grand Rapids, MI: Eerdmans, 1989), 194-196.

128. In Hebrews 11, the writer of Hebrews frames faith as a biographical rather than purely doctrinal apprehension—a look to the embodied lives of faith of the patriarchs and prophets of old that have created a tradition of lived faith upon which we now stand. This great "cloud of witnesses" provides a depository of faith that we're reminded of and hence remembered by, pulled together and woven into the tapestry of their stories lived through us.

It is just their Jobs and Hamlets that are not dreamt of in philosophies which rule out from the company of true being whatever cannot be numbered or included in an impersonal pattern. Drama and epic set forth pattern too, but it is one of personal relations. Hence we may call internal history dramatic and its truth dramatic truth, though drama in this case does not mean fiction.[129]

Niebuhr continues this idea by suggesting that our internal history and the history of the world, particularly God's history, are correlated:

> To be a self is to have a god; to have a god is to have a history, that is, events connected in a meaningful pattern; to have one God is to have one history. God and the history of the selves in community belong together in inseparable union [. . .] the God who is found in inner history, or rather who reveals himself there, is not the spiritual life but universal God, the creator not only of the events through which he discloses himself but also of all other happenings. The standpoint of the Christian community is limited, being in history, faith, and sin. But what is seen from this standpoint is unlimited.[130]

Writer and theologian Eugene Peterson suggests that life "is not managing a religious business but a spiritual quest."[131] Yet without the challenge of the quest, many in our society settle for the pithy and the quaint rather than the mystery and the wonder that's the fullness of the life poetic in God.

We're members of a disillusioned society. People in Western culture have been force-fed bumper-sticker slogans for the past five decades and lost their sense of spiritual mooring, both in regard to community and themselves. Pop psychology has

---

129. Niebuhr, "The Story of Our Life," 35.

130. Ibid., 38.

131. Eugene Peterson, *Reality and the Vision*, ed. Philip Yancey (Waco, TX: Word Publishing, 1990), 20.

stripped much of the dynamic flesh from our humanity, yet it's merely a symptom of a deeper societal sickness—fear.

The drive in modernity for control, clarity, and ease, often manifested in cold rationalism or high-minded atheism, is in some respects merely the mirror of many postmodern attempts, through irrationalism and relativism, to embrace pointless entertainment and sell it as play (which, as we've already learned, is not what Jerome Berryman views as Godly Play—something that is always deeply purposeful and certainly not trivial) over progress. Granted, there are many helpful, constructive renderings of modern and postmodern critiques. However, in some of the expressions of modernity and postmodernity, what we are left with are essentially shadow selves of each other in their respective disillusionment that comes from a loss of this "middle perspective."

Yet if we situate our uncertainty in the tension, if we strive for faith rather than propositions, and if we embrace our suffering not in isolation but in communion with our brothers and sisters, we'll reside in the uneasy yet necessary middle perspective of humility, welcoming grace, and mercy

In John Boorman's 1981 film *Excalibur*, which is based on Malory's *Le Morte d'Arthur*, the Grail quest of Sir Perceval is exemplified as a narrative that demonstrates the true integration of our lives that's to be found in the quest. At the point of his greatest despair in searching for the Holy Grail, Sir Perceval beholds a vision that will direct him to the resting place of the Grail. With this beatific illumination, Perceval is reminded of the integration of all things in the healing of the broken land and the dying King Arthur:

> **GRAIL FIGURE:** What is the secret of the Grail? Who does it serve?
> **PERCEVAL:** You, my lord.
> **GRAIL FIGURE:** Who am I?

PERCEVAL: You are my lord and king. You are Arthur.
GRAIL FIGURE: Have you found the secret that I have lost?
PERCEVAL: Yes. You and the land are one.[132]

This unity of all things—the integration of particular life stories into the grand narrative of all things for the healing and redemption of both self and world—is the summative attainment of the quest narrative. It's the acknowledgment that the healing of one will in part be the healing of many—the land and the king are one—that offers a powerful reminder as to the role that our particular stories will play as they become interwoven into the lives of others. Similarly, the context for the healing and redemption of the world is in part not necessarily far off. As with the illumination of Perceval, it's never what we've lost but what we've forgotten that becomes vital in the life poetic.

In Luke 22:19-20, when Jesus gathers his disciples together in the upper room and institutes the Eucharist, he does so through binding himself to the Passover as its source and substance by stating, "This is my body given for you. . . . This cup is the new covenant in my blood, which is poured out for you." He moves into the space of salvation for our world intimately rather than merely being a spectator.

As Christ pours himself out into this, he calls the disciples to now do this work as well in verse 19: "Do this in remembrance of me." This type of work—do this—is rendered in the Greek as *poiete*—the word that is the cognate for our English term *poetry*. This is a deeply creative term that goes to the heart of what it means for us to be God's people in these dark and desperate times. This is our identity in the world as we hear in Ephesians 2:10, "For we are God's handiwork [*poiete*], created in Christ Jesus, to do good works, which God prepared in

---

132. *Excalibur* (1981), directed by John Boorman. Internet Movie Database: www.imdb.com/title/tt0082348/quotes.

advance for us to do." At the very heartbreaking reality of who we are—we're called to a life of direction, release, and ultimate integration with our Creator—a poetic integration that's prepared in advance for us to do. This is what it means to be on the quest and embrace the life poetic.

At the beginning of this chapter, I discussed the danger in dismissing too readily a narrative approach to our lives and thereby dismissing the deep narrative of the Scriptures that seek to form and transform our lives. Author and pastor Frederick Buechner brings this thought full circle:

> If we think the purpose of Jesus' stories is essentially to make a point as extractable as a moral at the end of a fable, then the inevitable conclusion is that once you get the point, you can throw away the story itself like the rind of an orange when you have squeezed out the juice. Is that true? Or is the story itself the point and truth of the story? Is the point of Jesus' stories that they point to the truth about you and me and our stories? [. . .] The truth of the story is not a motto suitable for framing. It is a truth that one way or another, God help us, we live out every day of our lives. It is a truth as complicated and sad as you and I ourselves are complicated and sad, and as joyous and as simple as we are too. The stories that Jesus tells us are about us. Once upon a time is our time, in other words.[133]

The story is our story, yours and mine, youth group leader and youth. As Perceval understands through his beatific vision, our lives, our stories, are intimately interwoven into the stories of this world. The healing of the world in part begins with the healing and redemption that is readily at hand in our own lives and then committed to the world as confession and testimony. Additionally, unless we are willing to deeply read the life poetic that we and those around us have been given, we'll

---

133. Buechner, *The Clown in the Belfry*, 309–310.

be left only with a shadowy tale without flesh and blood. This is a challenge to our reading of Scripture as well. On one level, it's about a man with an ark, a man interpreting dreams for a king, a pearl of great price being found in a field, a woman who receives the word that she will give birth to the living Word, a man lost beside a pool who has found his sight, and young English schoolchildren asleep in the mane of a lion in a land with an ever-lit lamppost and a broken stone table. On the other hand, it's about faith, miracles seen and unseen, reaching out to a neighbor, and glimpsing God with eyes of childlike wonder. As Mark put it, "He did not say anything to them without using a parable" (Mark 4:34). In looking at the power of Christ's ministry as a life poetic, it's small wonder he communicated so much in narrative.

As Jeremy said on that dock at camp as we mused about how literature can show the way, the power of the gospel narrative is to provide more than merely a map. Instead, it's to be a true guide for the quest that is our lives. The literature teenagers are delving into in their classes, in their reading clubs over the summer, and what they are poring over on the bus is often shaping a world of possibilities that's providing some sense of direction, release, and integration. True, some of the dystopian fantasy that fills up the YA bookshelves is dark and brooding. But this also speaks to a deep hunger teenagers have to find resources for their quest for meaning, and it mirrors the darkness that's just below the surface of many teens. Here's an opportunity to engage teens like Jeremy in a conversation that has already begun. Find out what the young people you work with are reading and ask them what animates them as they turn the pages. The quest they're on in these narratives will provide exciting opportunities to blur the lines between the protagonists and plots they enjoy and are challenged by with the grand narrative of faith in the way of Jesus. Jesus' life and ministry was so large and meaningful that no one book could ever contain it, for, as we read in John 21:25, "If every one of them were written down, I suppose that even the whole world would not have room for the books that would be written."

CHAPTER 8

BLURRING
IMAGES
Coming of Age in Transformative Videos
and Films

In working with young people . . . do not try to call them back to where they were, and do not try to call them to where you are, beautiful as that place may seem to you. You must have the courage to go with them to a place where neither you nor they have been before.[134]

The gospel always comes to people in cultural robes. There is no such thing as a "pure" gospel, isolated from culture. [135]

In the previous chapter we looked at how narrative found in fiction provides resources for youth to find direction, release, and integration through youth culture. Through fantasy literature such as Harry Potter, The Hunger Games, and other examples in fiction, young people continually find resources to engage the deep hunger of their hearts and souls—those "secret

---

134. Vincent J. Donovan, *Christianity Rediscovered: An Epistle from the Masai* (London: SCM, 1982), vii.

135. David J. Bosch, *Transforming Mission: Paradigm Shifts in Theology of Mission* (London: Orbis Books, 1991), 297.

caverns" that St. Augustine challenges us to discover even in the midst of an ever-changing, constantly moving culture. Yet the world of youth culture is dominated by visual as well as written means to engage and enliven youth.

One of the interesting shifts in youth culture is the rise of the image as a chronicle of development of the self. Instagram has eclipsed Facebook for many young people as a social networking platform in part due to its ease of access, but also due to its focus on the image as the core means of marking life moments. The posting of "selfies" (pictures taken of oneself with a phone or tablet) have become a means of bookmarking experiences in time and place. Posting short videos on Vine, Vimeo, and YouTube are quick ways to connect groups of young people to events almost instantly. More and more young people are accessing video clips of films, television shows, and sporting events as opposed to watching the entire show—getting the highlights and key moments without the whole narrative. With these multiple means of accessing video and images, the narrative power of film and video continues to shape young people in powerful ways.

COMING-OF-AGE (INTERNAL) AND TRANSFORMATION (EXTERNAL AND COMMUNITY) FILMS

Two genres of film are vital toward understanding youth culture: The first are coming-of-age films, which have their roots in the *Bildungsroman* tradition of literature from the eighteenth and nineteenth centuries. The second are transformation films that deal primarily with the integration of teens into a sense of community and therefore focus primarily on the external environment.

According to Marc Swales, the *Bildungsroman* tradition is one in which "a regulated development within the life of the adolescent is observed, each of its stages has its own intrinsic value and is at the same time the basis for a higher stage. The dissonance and conflicts of life appear as the necessary growth points through which the individual must pass on his way to maturity and harmony."[136] Put another way, this is a long tradition in literature that's now being seen in film and video as well, of showing the young what it looks like to grow up and make good decisions as opposed to poor ones. Ultimately, it challenges young people to act out a life worthy of an adult for the sake of the world.

What differentiates the *Bildungsroman* genre from other forms of artistic representation is a stage of development that occurs *within* the life of the young adult. In similar strains to the faith developmental theories of James Fowler, James Loder, and Sharon Daloz Parks, where other forms of artistic displays of one's coming-of-age process have an external locus of movement and action, the true action is of an *internal* focus that takes place within the character and soul of the adolescent, rather than through external events. The message inherent to this genre is that there is meaning to life and that as one exits the final stages of adolescence, one should keep his or her eyes open and the mind awake, for it is in this twilight time between adolescence and adulthood that deep meaning and lasting elements of character are revealed.

Also, there's a stage-by-stage development that's seen through the life of the *Bildungsroman* hero where causal connections are made building toward a "moment of illumination" and personal reckoning. *Who am I? Who am I to be in the world?* In distilling the *Bildungsroman* genre, one can find a very common framework throughout:

---

136. Martin Swales, *The German Bildungsroman from Wieland to Hesse* (Princeton, NJ: Princeton University Press, 1978), 3.

1. The presentation of an adolescent who is representative of his or her own generation who determines how and why either to rebel against the previous generation or conform to it.
2. The adolescent hero's negative response to formal education highlights his or her individuality and creates problems for ultimate integration into society at large.
3. There is a journey to the urban center of the city, which introduces the adolescent to "real life," where he or she confronts the following two problems:
   a. Encounters with good and evil through which he or she formulates his or her moral or ethical code
   b. Encounters with sex or love, which reflect his or her developing maturity
4. The economic background of the adolescent determines how he or she will view his or her experiences.
5. The use of a guide or mentor for the adolescent reveals his or her level of self-determination in that it shows his or her ability to accept guidance.
6. The ending places the adolescent hero on the verge of adulthood through a revelation or insight that follows from all of the above.

A contemporary example of this is seen in the life of Katniss Everdeen, the heroine of Suzanne Collins' YA novel *The Hunger Games*. Katniss is a sixteen-year-old girl who is trying to survive in a war-ravaged, post-apocalyptic America, now called Panem. Every year the citizens' children are forced to participate in an annual contest where two adolescents, or tributes, from each of the twelve districts of Panem are selected to battle to the death. In the novels as well as the film versions, Katniss represents a classic *Bildungsroman* heroine: She offers herself as a tribute in place of her younger sister, and she journeys from poverty to the grand Capitol where she's put on display and tempted to follow the rules of a corrupt system. As in the tradition of the *Bildungsroman*, she makes decisions about good versus evil, whether she will fall in love, and whether or not to follow the advice of mentors.

More and more films are returning to this model of storytelling, which speaks to our culture's desire to tell stories that form, shape, and release young people into society with resources to succeed. The explosion of growth in young adult–themed fiction and films in the past few decades demonstrates that teens desire role models and larger-than-life stories to aspire to; and the culture is responding by offering young people books, music, film, videos, and myriad resources to accommodate this hunger. What's also important to note is that while mass media surrounds and envelopes teens in ways that are unparalleled, the stories from which young people draw meaning and by which they are shaped into adulthood continue to draw from old time-tested sources, such as the quest narrative we discussed in the previous chapter and the *Bildungsroman*, or coming-of-age, stories. This means that generations have connections, share stories, and are not as different in what it means to come of age as we might think. Of course Katniss Everdeen in *The Hunger Games*, Benson Fisher in *Variant*, and Beatrice Prior in *Divergent* are new characters, but their type is rather old, as we shall see.

The movement of the adolescent in the *Bildungsroman* genre is ultimately a move from a sense of estrangement and isolation (referencing Chap Clark's use of the term "abandonment") in an accelerated culture to a grounding in and through the trials of life with the guidance of significant mentors. Ministry in today's youth culture has as one of its central tasks that of providing tools and encouragement for overcoming the sense of isolation of today's youth—helping them move toward intimacy with Christ and a call to a faith continually formed through gracious service to others. The danger is in providing only techniques for ministry to youth and forgoing the call to mentor our students through embodied example. As Jacques Ellul prophetically stated back in 1964:

> Technique [in and of itself] has become a reality in itself, self-sufficient, with its special laws and its own determinations. Let us not deceive ourselves on this point . . . Technique tolerates no judgment from without and accepts no limitation . . . The power and autonomy of technique are so well secured that it, in its turn, has become the judge of what is moral, the creator of a new morality. Thus, it plays the role of creator of a new civilization as well.[137]

Authentic ministry to youth deserves more than statistics and technique that are merely *transactional* education. Here's a call to a deeper notion of ministerial formation that is *transformational*. In the return to narrative forms of evangelism (for example, the national reinterpretation of evangelism by Youth for Christ as "the gift of story"), the narrative of coming-of-age as a confessional process of becoming is indeed meaningful. As we approach recorded events in our lives—even our recorded lives—it's important to approach them as a narrative akin to the *Bildungsroman*, or else we face the grievous view of life being a series of meaninglessly strung-together footprints in the sands of time.

THE COMING-OF-AGE OF ANAKIN SKYWALKER IN STAR WARS

One of the most enduring movie franchises in recent history has been the Star Wars series—it has continued long after the first series of films in the forms of an animated series, books, comics, and other cultural resources. Much of the series and its

---

137. Jacques Ellul, *The Technology Society* (New York: Vintage Books, 1964), 134.

metamyth has spawned further science fiction films, and decades after the first films were projected on the screen, it remains the source of both adoration and parody and continues to be a source of conversation even among young people today. In *Episode I: The Phantom Menace*, Anakin (whose story unfolds with Christological echoes as he is born a slave and his mother is supposedly a virgin) grows and develops through his encounter with his environment. As he's trained, he's encouraged to focus on his "destiny" rather than a systematic shaping of a *tabula rasa*. As Yoda mentions, although he is "the Chosen One who will bring balance to the Force," he also is one whose "future is clouded."[138]

Anakin is change incarnate, but he's change with meaning and purpose. To use language more germane to theological reflection, Anakin has been given the dignity of free will even amidst the grand eschatological destiny that surrounds him. His mother, the Virgin Mary-esque Shmi Skywalker, muses aphoristically, "You can't stop change any more than you can stop the suns from setting."[139] In line with the coming-of-age pattern, he journeys away from his rural background, becomes enlightened through education and training as a Jedi, moves among the powerful and elite of society, falls in love, and ultimately renounces his calling by leaving his true identity behind and embracing the literal and figurative mask of Darth Vader. The archetype of Darth Vader in relation to his (spoiler alert!) son Luke Skywalker fuels and frames the coming-of-age story in that while the father (Anakin) strays from the path, it's the son (Luke) who stays true to his calling to the very end, and his faithfulness will lead to the redemption of the generations to follow.

---

138. Internet Movie Database, Biography for Yoda, http://www.imdb.com/character/ch0000015/bio.

139. *Star Wars Episode I: The Phantom Menace* (1999); www.imdb.com/title/tt0120915/quotes.

The power of this type of film should be fairly clear: to "come of age" isn't merely for one's personal actualization—rather it's for the sake of others. These kinds of films also demonstrate that whether you come from a poor and disadvantaged background or a wealthy and supportive community, whether your family system is flawed and broken or loving and whole, every young person must choose an inner vision for his or her life and then live according to that vision regardless of the circumstances.

TRANSFORMATION FILMS

Transformation films focus on the transformation of a main character and the integration of that character into a true community of support. As with most films in youth culture, the focus on the self is in line with coming-of-age films, but with the distinction of seeing transformation through the lens of external contexts: family, friends, school, church, or other factors. At the beginning of these films, the main character is portrayed as oppressed, unattractive, or unhappy. Slowly, through the recognition of others and themselves, these characters blossom and transform into attractive, glowing, talented extroverts who become recognized as insiders by the community. Characteristics of these films include the following:

- Exaggerated nerdiness, awkwardness, and unattractiveness in the beginning, followed by exaggerated popularity, grace, and beauty at the end.
- Some sort of grand ceremony where the person emerges in front of old friends and foes as a new and better self.
- A pervasive idea that once physical perfection is attained, mental health, self-esteem, and inner peace will automatically follow. This is the idea of finding one's "true identity."
- Old and new identities of protagonists rely on a rigid and stereotypical social structure where there are strict cat-

egories of people including nerds, jocks, beauty queens, smart people. The emergence of a new identity usually relies on this social structure in order to define itself.

- Sometimes the main character attains influential power at the end and "opens people's eyes" to the way they treat others.
- School is usually the primary setting.
- An "unlikely" romance between a nerd and a popular character is common.
- The protagonist is often "discovered" and helped by either someone in the popular, talented, and beautiful crowd, or a mentor.
- Parents, siblings, and families are usually not as emphasized or as important as peer groups.

Films that fall into this category are plentiful: *The Breakfast Club, The Karate Kid, Some Kind of Wonderful, The Princess Diaries, She's All That*, the High School Musical series, and *Pitch Perfect*, just to name a few. In regard to *Pitch Perfect* and the television show *Glee*, another concept that these films offer is the power of music and finding your "voice" in concert with others as a means of transformation. (We'll look closely at the power of music in youth culture in the next chapter.)

One of the recent areas that transformation films have grown in is the way in which popularity is counterpointed with notions of nerdiness and geek culture. In most transformation films, being popular and part of the in crowd is initially alluring. Yet what's quickly revealed is that popularity is competitive, whereas nerd and geek culture is cooperative. The success of the individual in transformation films is about finding the right group and becoming a champion for that group through thick and thin. Where the traditional coming-of-age narrative is about the singular person standing tall in a crowd, the transformation film is about the group standing tall together before a crowd of competitive individuals who lack the trust and intimacy of the group.

THE VIEWING OF FILM AS BLUR

It's important to note that critically watching film is an art that takes work, and this is something young people need mentorship in as much as any academic subject. Since they're inundated with media sources all day, helping them develop tools of discernment for how to "read" film is critical. We can fall into the lazy habit of merely "viewing," and film can seem like something we can just take in without struggling to improve our understanding.

In a critical scene from the 1986 film *Ferris Bueller's Day Off*, Ferris, Cameron, and Sloane have skipped school for the day. As part of their adventures in Chicago, they make a stop at the Art Institute. Through a visual montage as the teens wander from exhibit to exhibit, Cameron becomes fixated on a little girl in Georges Seurat's famous painting *A Sunday Afternoon on the Island of La Grande Jatte*. As this scene unfolds, viewers are caught watching Cameron . . . well . . . staring. We go from jump cut of the painting to Cameron's eyes, focusing ever deeper on specifics of the painting and becoming more and more entranced. We're drawn closer and closer to the canvas, and what was once a large scene by the lake becomes an examination of intense detail. This is instructive for us: if we stare too intensely at details, we can lose the big picture altogether. We look at a painting like Cameron does or the film of Cameron staring at the painting as if in a hall of mirrors, and we're always reflecting on where we are and where this painting is and came from. But films are different from static images. The cinematic image is a moving one, and much like the blurring of categories and meanings that constitute teenagers in our culture, we need to consider how to not only stare at films, but instead we must learn to truly read and reflect, seeing deeply with a critical turn.

In short, to read film is to first accept the fact that it's not a passive enterprise, but that shouldn't take the joy out of it. Merely "viewing" any image is ultimately a form of both idolatry (passively becoming the object rather than the subject) and iconoclasm (seeing only the surface and not into the depth of a thing is ultimately to destroy it). This is the task of religion and the call of people of faith.[140]

We know the power of certain images to hold sway over the imagination. Mass media outlets mediate through and with images: We're expected to understand the meaning of the void created in the New York skyline after September 11, and the toppling of Saddam's image in central Baghdad played over and over on television screens. We know at an innate level that something is going on when certain images hit us—their power to embody and make present the very being of their object. Profound responses in the presence of images (desire, fear) transcend the sorts of boundaries that academics establish between the canon of so-called "high art" folk and tribal arts, popular logos from Starbucks to Nike, and the devotional images found in our places of worship. *Film is a medium of immediate imaging. Where some images and texts require some reflection and repose prior to understanding, most film demands and receives an immediate reaction and understanding.* It displays a world much more convincingly and immediately than any other symbolic form. As mechanical reproduction, it gives the illusion of pure reference. As a moving picture, it seems to offer an ongoing experience of time present and therefore of presence.

---

140. Babara De Concini, "Seduction by Visual Image," *The Journal of Religion and Film* 2(3) (December 1998), section 1.

THREE POINTERS FOR READING FILM

Barbara De Concini has three pointers for learning to read video, whether it's in a theater, on a flat screen in your living room, or on our laptap or tablet.[141] These are suggestions for you to put into practice during the next film event you have with teenagers. Since the viewer tends to identify with the camera's lens as the authoritative angle of value to be considered (which is roughly equivalent to the point of view in a novel), we should school ourselves to pay attention to the camera. De Concini suggests the following:

1. Pay attention to how the camera frames and holds the subject.

    How much of the human figure is in view—how much of the surroundings? What happens to our perceptions when the character is presented to us in extreme long shot (a mere speck on the screen) as opposed to in extreme close-up where the individual face can become a whole spiritual landscape? An image in painting or a photograph can be rich with symbolic import, but it must achieve its effects within the frame. A movie is a moving picture, a multiplicity of frames—astoundingly, as many as 180,000 in a two-hour film.

2. Watch the camera's angle of vision.

    The angle from which a subject is photographed has an impact on how the image reads. As Louis Giannetti demonstrates in *Understanding Movies*, an eye-level shot suggests parity between viewer and subject. High angles reduce the subject's significance, suggesting vulnerability; and low angles do the opposite, creating a sense of dominance over the viewer.

3. Remember that camera shots tend to acquire meaning when they are seen in relation to other shots.

    The images and ideas exist within the film, but meaning also comes from the associations the viewer brings. This is

---

141. Babara De Concini, "Seduction by Visual Image," section 1.

one of the most characteristic ways in which the cinematic image expresses the "something more." We can call it symbolic, but, as people who are used to the written text, our expectations of the symbolic may mislead us. Here the process is often a quite humble one that falls into a sort of middle range of meaning between the immediacy of the iconic and the latency of the symbolic. Through editing, the filmmaker elaborates visually on some natural links and fairly straightforward connections, piecing together sets of visual associations, pattering thematic and metaphorical affinities for us through the iterative process of the cinema.

These three pointers for viewing videos and film provide a great tool by which to actively engage teenagers in the task of what they are viewing, what the producer of the media they are consuming is offering, and an active call to critique that which is being viewed based on the values, morals, ethics, and core faith they bring to the media. This is a great exercise for families to engage in as well. I've challenged parents in youth ministries in the past to take a one-week media audit with their teen and use these three pointers in relation to what they think God's point of view on the subjects in the video or film is. Does God frame men and women in the way the director has done in sexually explicit ways? Does the angle of the camera make us feel small and diminished or perhaps overly exalted? As the scenes cut and jump cut between plot points, what in real life is getting edited out? What's the down time that's left on the cutting room floor, and is that a part of our lives that God would edit out? These kinds of conversations actively engage teenagers in media critique that isn't necessarily setting up their favorite television show as all bad. Rather, it allows teens to demonstrate that some of the ways mass media portrays things is problematic in relation to how God wishes creation to be seen and experienced. And it also allows teens to show that even in shows that deal with difficult subject matter, such as sex and drugs, God can be recalled and perhaps even acknowledged.

This was evident when I discussed the 2012 film *Pitch Perfect* with a group of students. This movie is about a group of college students who are social misfits yet find community and meaning as part of an a capella singing group. The plot is fairly standard and the resolution to the narrative is pretty textbook (spoiler alert: the boy and girl get together in the end, and there's a big musical number). But as we walked through the film critically, the students picked up on themes and points they hadn't previously considered.

For example, this movie is typical in its jump cutting from one romantic moment to the next plot point without any space in between for conversation, disagreement, or even time for the relationship to truly gel. I asked the students how this affected the way they saw romantic relationships. They all agreed that the speed to resolution of conflict found in films and television makes it difficult to be patient—the jump cuts in real life just don't happen. Yet they also noted that while people can write off the notion of people just breaking into song and dance, there's something to that moment of transcendence that related to how they felt in relation to faith. It also resonated with how they felt life *should* be—young people want to live life like that and actually wish they had more role models who lived lives abandoned to passion and joy.

DESIRE AND THE QUEST FOR GOD

The desire that life showed more passion is key to James K. A. Smith's work, in particular the first volume of his Cultural Liturgies series titled *Desiring the Kingdom: Worship, Worldview, and Cultural Formation*, where he makes the point that rather than seeing human beings as merely thinking, rational beings (which is so indicative of the academic enterprise we often resource our reflections on youth culture), we need to see humans as *Homo Liturgicus* or "the human person as lover." Smith says,

> We need a nonreductionistic understanding of human persons as embodied agents of desire and love. . . . The point is to emphasize that the way we inhabit the world is not primarily as thinkers, or even as believers, but as more affective, embodied creatures who make our way in the world more by feeling our way around it. . . . One might say that in our everyday mundane being-in-the-world, we don't lead with our head, so to speak; we lead out with our heart and hands.[142]

This is behind much of the love story motifs that populate many of the shows teenagers watch and stream on their phones, iPads, Kindles, and laptops. Teens are actively engaged with the quest for purpose, and ultimately this is also a quest for and in response to desire and love.

In a sermon titled "The Depth of Experience," theologian Paul Tillich supports Smith's claim that we're people formed by and for desire when he states that desire marks one of the essential aspects of our humanity and is one of the evidences of the *Imago Dei*: the Image of God. For Tillich, our desire for what's "truly desirable" drives so much of our activity, and we can certainly see how and why visual culture is consumed with provoking desire in young people. Tillich goes on to note that it's desiring and finding disappointments in this life that "the truth of which does not disappoint dwells below the surface in the depth."[143] Here Tillich sees depth as that meaning-making encounter that evidences our meeting with the divine or as Tillich states, "the name of this infinite and inexhaustible depth

142. James K. A. Smith, *Desiring the Kingdom: Worship, Worldview, and Cultural Formation* (Grand Rapids, MI: Baker Books, 2009), 47.

143. Paul Tillich, *The Shaking of the Foundations* (New York: Charles Scribner's, 1948), 53.

and ground of all being is God. That depth is what the word *God* means."[144]

To see the issues of love and desire which populate much of the media that teenagers consume as being, in part, a quest to reconnect with who we are as desiring, loving beings created in and for the *Imago Dei* is a powerful reminder to those who work with youth to not be too quick to dismiss romantic comedies as mere distraction or pulp entertainment. Even shows with questionable morals like *Pretty Little Liars*, based on Sara Shepard's YA novels, offers a window into a hunger for love and connection, which can be a launching pad for deeper conversations about what it means to love and desire as people made in the image of God.

As we are called to mentor and lead young people through this process of becoming, it's not enough to merely provide a map of self-actualization framed by our own life experience, nor will it work to borrow the hagiography of others. As we see in the process of the *Bildungsroman* as it's reborn in the cinematic possible futures of coming-of-age and transformation films, to become a mature self isn't about finding the perfect map: some objectified set of rules for the game of life. Rather, it's about finding and walking alongside a worthy guide. The cry of today's youth sitting in our movie theaters is not one of merely becoming—but becoming *with*. That is to say, becoming a person of communion *with* others—to be seen as one alongside those who have gone before them and those who will follow. Our ministry is a challenge of being fully present as incarnated realities of mercy and grace. It's through presences and intimacy alongside the sojourn of youth into adulthood that we as mentors can also overturn the power of falsehood found in some films and reveal the true image of Christ. As we discussed in chapter 4, this theology of intimacy is proclaimed by Jesus in Mark 10:14-16:

---

144. Tillich, *The Shaking of the Foundations*, 57.

"Let the little children come to me, and do not hinder them, for the kingdom of God belongs to such as these. Truly I tell you, anyone who will not receive the kingdom of God like a little child will never enter it." And he took the children in his arms, placed his hands on them and blessed them.

To deny this calling of intimacy and presence and allow young people of this age to wander blithely between destiny and chance is to deserve the indignation Jesus feels toward the disciples in Mark 10:14. We've been called to much more than getting our theology right—we've been called to walk through these slender threads of becoming with those God desires to draw close.

CHAPTER 9

BLURRING
SOUND

The Rise of the Sonic Mystic in Youth Culture

As we approached the dawn of the twenty-first century, Loren Mead of the Alban Institute made the following pronouncement: "The storm buffeting the churches is very serious indeed . . . so serious that it marks the end of 'business as usual' for the churches and marks the need for us to begin again building the church from the ground up."[145] Now that we're into this millennia, we can see that Mead's pronouncement back in 1994 was prophetic. The notion of "business as usual" for what it means to be a church has certainly changed. The age of globalized media; radical shifts in church attendance in mainline denominations; the rise and decline of evangelicalism; and the ways majority world leaders and theologians from Africa, Latin America, Eastern Europe, and Asia have all seen surges in church membership (notably among younger people) show us that we're in an age where "the need for us to begin again building the church from the ground up" is upon us all.

145. Loren B. Mead, *Transforming Congregations for the Future* (Herndon, VA: The Alban Institute, 1994), ix.

One of the things we can be assured of is the degree to which God is doing just that: building the church from the ground up and doing so through the culture in which young people are meeting the Lord in exciting ways. There is a new spiritual openness today. As noted in a study done in the UK by David Hay and Kate Hunt, research suggests that people today are 60 percent more likely to speak about a spiritual experience than they were in the previous century.[146] This is exemplified in the studies we've reflected on thus far from the NSYR, as well as the work of Jerome Berryman and others. For those who are deeply concerned about the next generation and the communities of faith in which they will find a sense of home, part of a renewed missiological approach should be to offer a context for spiritual exploration and quest, a place of intimacy and openness to questions. One way to respond to this openness is what St. Augustine challenges us with in chapter 6 in relation to youth culture being a place where one can actually find God at work, not merely a place to keep young people from engaging.

Thus far we have engaged the way young people experience God through the narratives that shape them. In literature and films young people are equipped with a vision of direction, release, and integration through a calling of the grand quest of faith. Through mentorships in deeply committed communities, young people are given the resources to find character, become convicted of God's call on their lives, and live into the abiding community of disciples and fellow sojourners to sustain that journey. Another way young people engage God in the culture in which they live, move, and have their being is through music.

---

146. David Hay and Kate Hunt, *Understanding the Spirituality of People Who Don't Go to Church: A Report on the Findings of the Adults' Spirituality Project at the University of Nottingham* (August 2000), spiritualjourneys.org.uk.

THE SONIC MYSTIC

In an earlier book I wrote about the nature of popular music as it relates to the Christian virtues of faith, hope, and love, I reflected on the nature of sound and how music forms a connection with God in ways that are both acknowledged and yet to be discovered.[147] Much of the consumption of popular music today evidences a hunger to connect with that aspect of life that lives beyond the ordinary and pushes us into the realm of the transcendent. Whether it's the crush of the crowd at a rock concert as we sing along to a well-known anthem with 60,000 other fans, or as we sit in solitude with our iPods listening to a plaintive ballad that digs deep into our most raw longings and hopes, music connects us to what it means to be alive. For many young people, it's also the medium that expresses their sense of spiritual longing and celebration in ways that mere text can't do.

In studying young people and reflecting on their hunger for meaning through popular music, I've seen over and over again that the way in which they frequently connect with music is not mere consumerism alone, but it's what the mystical tradition has always done. This is in many ways a generation of what I term "sonic mystics"—those who find meaning in popular music through its power to release them from that which binds them and prevents them from transcendence (what the mystics term *purgation*), as a way to shine a light on both the things of life that are reflective of God and those things that are devoid of the grace of God (what the mystics term *illumination*), and ultimately as a means of marking out the memories and form of what intimacy with God and others can be (what the mystics call *union*).

For centuries, there has been the view that to move in the resonant frequency of the living God is to be emptied,

---

147. Jeffrey F. Keuss, *Your Neighbor's Hymnal: What Popular Music Teaches Us about Faith, Hope, and Love* (Eugene, OR: Cascade Books, 2011).

awakened, and united in relationship as this three-fold movement of continuous purgation, illumination, and union.[148] Young people get this, and perhaps it's now time for the wider church to get it as well.

PURGATION: TO BE EMPTIED SO THAT WE HEAR ANEW

Music encounters us as an act of forgetting and release into new ways of being before it's anything else. Think of a time when you first heard a song that grabbed your attention so fully that you stopped what you were doing and lost yourself in the song. I remember driving home one evening when a song came on the radio that not only had I never heard before, but I needed to know what it was because it knocked my socks off. I pulled into a 7-Eleven parking lot and just sat there until the song was over so I could find out what it was. Before that song came on, my mind was filled with thoughts about work, picking up the groceries, what I was going to do with friends that night. All those thoughts just disappeared within the space of a four-minute pop song. I sat in a parking lot with my car's engine running, people were coming and going with Slurpees in their hands, but I wasn't there anymore—I was "in" the song as it moved, collapsed, gained energy, and resolved into a new verse.

---

148. Cf. John Cassian (360–435) in his two major works: *The Institutes* (Latin: *De institutis coenobiorum*), which deals with the external organization of monastic communities and how communities form, and *The Conferences* (Latin: *Collationes*), which deals with the training of the inner person and the perfection of the heart. These stages of being emptied, awakened, and united in relationship are later articulated by St. John of the Cross (1542–1591), a Spanish Carmelite monk whose key works such as *The Spiritual Canticles* and *The Dark Night of the Soul* exemplify the Gospel accounts of moving from darkness into light in passages such as Matthew 4:1-11; Mark 1:12-13; and Luke 4:1-13.

When the song was done, it was as if I awoke in a new place not knowing how I got there.

For the mystics, this is the movement of purgation or *purgatio*. In this stage a person is brought to awareness that they're not fully present to themselves or to the world around them and something has to give. Think of this as a cold splash of water to the face, tripping over your own feet, or—in the case of the sonic mystic—a song that breaks through all the emotional and spiritual static that clouds our hearts and minds and brings forth that resonant frequency of pure meaning. In the mystical tradition of the Christian, this is when someone struggles to gain control of "the flesh"—specifically gluttony, lust, and the desire for possessions in hopes of finding meaning and purpose beyond such things.

For the sonic mystic who trolls through digital downloads on their media player or through the bins of the used record store, it's a similar search for a shock, a slap, a push to move beyond all the crash and bang of meaninglessness and vibrate with the frequency that moved the planets and stars from the beginning of time. This attempt at emptying oneself of that which crowds out meaning, depth, and purpose is the same for both the Christian monk that St. John of the Cross wrote about so long ago and the pop song lover who wears headphones while sitting next to you on the bus.

It's important to note that this attempt to break the cycle of meaninglessness—both for the devout Carmelite monk and the pop music sonic mystic of the twenty-first century—occurs sometimes as an active purging and sometimes as an unplanned passive event. In the mystic tradition, this is twinned movement of active and passive purgation. Active purgation or intentional emptying is when the conscientious monk actively seeks release from that which clouds the *Imago Dei* (the Image of God) which is our true identity. The monk is made aware, whether through the counsel of a mentor or through deep prayer and study, that some things in the way we live our lives need to be changed in order to hear God anew. This active purgation can be times of silence, working at menial tasks that humble a person, or times of confession and seeking forgiveness to release those things that bind the heart and soul. Passive purgation or unintentional emptying of the soul occurs when we are confronted with events—or even music—that's surprising and therefore beyond our control.

These moments of passive purgation or unintentional emptying can feel like we've had our pocket picked: we might not notice what happened until we reach for what we think is there only to find that it's now gone. Or it can feel like having the wind knocked out of us when we trip, or maybe it's like being pulled underwater by an unseen, yet powerful, undertow. This can occur with joyful revelations of wonder and amazement, like when we meet someone with whom we instantly become smitten, or it can be through tragic events that thrust us into suffering or crisis. Whether it be joy or suffering, silence or the rhythmic beat of a snare drum, high-hat cymbal, and pulsing bass guitar, it's in the movement of emptying the soul that we can find that which we've held to be so vital, so important, so foundational to everything we guard as essential can be released. Only then can we become open to the possibility of new ways of being and, more importantly, new or renewed relationships that will bring us there.

ILLUMINATION: WHEN HEARING BECOMES SEEING ANEW

Once we've been struck by the new song, by the surprising new encounter of love, or the disappointment of loss through crisis, our resources by which we made sense of life become shifted.

The old songs just don't sound the same anymore; and we are drawn into the energy, the possibility, and the willingness to risk for something beyond that which had been. The "same old, same old" doesn't cut it any longer. It's at this point that the Christian mystics experience illumination or the *Illuminatio* of God in the form of communities. During this period the monk learned the paths to holiness revealed in the gospel story and sought to make sense of them in relation to other people. During the *Illuminatio* many monks took in visitors and students, and tended to the poor as much as their meager resources allowed.

For the sonic mystics, part of this journey can be seen as they move outside of themselves and deeper into following the artist's career that first set them on this journey of discovery: buying CDs and vinyl in the back catalog as a show of vintage support for music, seeking out the live shows, looking into the set lists of past concerts and how the artist has changed his or her music, and paying attention to when that artist is going back into the studio and what he or she is heading into next. This seeking after illumination is a seeking for something beyond us: that creative spark, the imagination that's aglow with possibilities, the drive to make something new in a world that's derivative.

Also, much of this journey of illumination for the sonic mystic is the discovery of the transcendent, which shapes the life of the everyday: things like love, caring, compassion, hope, faith, wonder, ecstasy, awe—things that can't be bottled or framed on the wall. Yet when these are sung, even within a pop song, for the briefest moment they carry us out of ourselves and bind us to the hearts of others.

For the Carmelite mystic following in the ways of St. John of the Cross, the essential desert island disc that no fanboy of God could go without was the life and teachings of Christ—in particular what Christ proclaimed as he taught the Sermon on the Mount, recounted in Matthew 5–7. The Christian monk continues a life of humility in the Spirit of God and stretches the self to be formed and reformed in relationship to others seeking a similar vision.

UNITY: WHEN LIFE SPENT STANDING AND FALLING IN THE MOSH PIT IS MORE THAN LIFE ON THE STAGE

The illumination stage for the sonic mystic takes him into the strangest place of all: a binding of his life to the lives of others. In this place he seeks to live life not as an individual but as a being who's part of something that makes sense only when it's shared with others. For the Christian mystic, this final stage is a stage of unity or *unitio*, a period when the soul of the monk and the Spirit of God are bonded together in a union often described as the marriage of the Song of Solomon (also called the Song of Songs or the Canticle of Canticles) because it's so intimate and core to what this new life that's forged after being emptied and coming into the new light of illumination.

For the sonic mystic, this journey begins with a sonic movement where the frequency of the soul resonates not only with the art that's drawing him higher and deeper, but also the community of others who share this journey. This unity with other people and the moment of music itself is most perfectly realized in the live performance. This is a moment of ecstatic union marked by ineffable joy, exaltation, and proclamation. Here's where we step outside of our small world of headphone speakers, the safety and isolation of our car, the cocoon of our private homes, and go out into the public space of the club, the stadium, or the open-air festival to meet the songs as they come alive not only from the artist, but in and through other fans who share this. This movement into the union is at once a proclamation, yet it's also ineffable and moves us beyond language itself.

One of the most famous ineffable screams in the U2 canon (cataloging these is a project we'll leave to another scholar) is found at 3:02 in "With or Without You" immediately following the lament that "you give yourself away / and you give / and you give / and you give yourself away" to the point of extinction, comes a wordless ecstatic release into mystical union as one is released from being outside of sound and becomes one with the sound itself. This is often fleeting in our lives—especially for the sonic mystic who finds these fleeting moments in the midst of a song that lasts only a few minutes. But in the community of fans, this moment continues on and on and on like a divine echo channeled down the canyons of culture.

This is the strange experience I continue to have at live shows as I'm pushed by other fans in the pulse of the music. We're at first unsure of each other—almost jealous of this music that's so close to us because we're unsure that anyone else gets it like we do. Then slowly as the show progresses, we forget ourselves and the music brings us together; and what was merely a collection of strangers becomes a sea of tuning forks resonating with the vibe, no longer caring who sees us singing along with these lyrics. At this moment we're not afraid that someone will think we're juvenile, and we can free-fall into the moment-by-moment movement of the show.

In rock shows you'll see stage diving and people surfing over your heads. In smaller venues with singer-songwriters, you'll see people tapping their feet with eyes fixed on a point beyond the artist and the stage to another time, another place. As people leave the live show, there's always a solemnity, an active yet quiet rush as the crowd hurries to beat traffic and get home before the evening turns to daylight. This solemnity after a live show has always hit me with a sense of remorse and sadness. Some will write off the live concert experience as escapism. Yet I have found the opposite. It's as if going back to our lives is entering the falsehood, and leaving the stadium, the club, or open-air festival is like being banished to live east of Eden for the remainder of our days.

Yet here is where the sonic mystic differs from many Christians in the new millennium in marked ways. As I watch people leave church after a Sunday service, there's almost a sense of relief—we've paid our dues to God, we sat through the worship service, and now we can get back to the business of living our lives for ourselves. It's this difference between what many Christians consider to be what the rest of our lives look like and what the sonic mystics understand as the role that the mystery, imagination, and transcendence of life that's only glimpsed at in a pop song. There's something lacking in many evangelical Christians' lives today—an energy, a playfulness, a willingness to weep when it's time to weep and laugh when it's time to laugh—that's still alive and well in the hearts, minds, and songs of the sonic mystics. It's their music that we need to listen to and their passion and commitment that needs to be taken seriously. For what is the worth of salvation if the life that's lived is so dead and our eyes so vacant that the so-called "Good News" that people see as they walk past a church parking lot on a Sunday morning seems to be, *Thank goodness that's over?*

THIS IS A CULTURE IN SEARCH OF TRANSCENDENCE AND INTIMACY THROUGH AN ELECTRONIC AND SONIC CULTURE[149]

My friend Peter Nielson has been a pastor in the Church of Scotland and a missionary to the club scene of Edinburgh. In some of his work with young people immersed in the music

---

149. Tex Sample, *The Spectacle of Worship in a Wired World: Electronic Culture and the Gathered People of God* (Nashville: Abingdon Press, 1998), 84.

scene, he has spelled out a way to reach out to a blurring culture
with these objectives:

Key Objectives

1. To establish authentic relationship with those who are part
   of the club scene.
2. To work as translators of Christianity to the club culture.
3. To set up a studio where musicians and artists can work
   together.
4. To develop a support network to identify the gifts, passions,
   dreams, frustrations, and pain of people in the club scene,
   and offer the appropriate practical/pastoral support.
5. To explore worship patterns that relate to the issues, sym-
   bols, music, and images of the club culture.
6. To develop a rhythm of life that will offer an accompanied
   path for those wanting to be followers of Jesus Christ.

What I love about how Peter approached his missional
task of reaching out to the music scene is that he readily
acknowledged that much of the music was simply not to his
taste or temperament. What mattered to the young people he
met in the clubs wasn't that he liked screamo or rave music—
what mattered was that he wanted to learn about the things
these young people loved. What gave them energy? How did
they feel alive as the bassline pulsed and beat against them
during a show? Practicing Augustine's notion that we're to
love that which those we love deem worth loving, Peter demonstrated over and over again that a middle-aged Church of
Scotland pastor can be a mentor and friend to young people
in a club.

When I asked Peter to share with my students at the University of Glasgow themes and approaches to ministry in the music
scene, he listed the following:

Core Themes

1. *A Culture of Learning.* We aim to create a gospel for the club culture by doing a visual diary of life in this context and reflecting together on that by living with a gospel for a year. This will be the basis of ongoing discipleship.
2. *Introduction and Induction.* We aim to help all who associate with the community to find their place within it.
3. *Communication.* We aim to develop regular email communication within the group, sustain links with the wider church, and draw on the wisdom of others beyond ourselves.

One of the passages of Scripture that Peter shared with me was Psalm 84 and what it means to be a "doorkeeper in the house of my God."[150] This was a vital teaching for Peter in his ministry within the music scene, and this acknowledges that those of us who hold power in the church need to move from blocking the doors to becoming doorkeepers who hold the doors open for a new generation to create church for that new generation—no more and no less.

DRAFTING A COVENANT IN WORKING WITH YOUNG PEOPLE IN THE ARTS

In working with young people in the arts scene, another important task is to make clear what your intentions are and how you wish to build relationships. Too often church folks have seen the missional task as a game of smoke and mirrors: wooing young people through promises of excitement and engagement with the literature, films, and music they love only to slam the door behind them and ask them to forsake all the culture that formed them in exchange for substitutes in the form of contemporary Christian music, Christian fiction, and Christian films.

150. Psalm 84:10

Is this truly the answer? This bait-and-switch approach has only alienated a culture from the church that has volumes to teach those who are willing to listen and learn.

In Peter's work with the club scene in Edinburgh, his ministry team drafted a "covenant with the missing generation"—a commitment to those young people who the church needs to listen to and learn from and who we—Christians seeking the future of God's kingdom—have been missing. Here's their covenant and something to consider drafting in your work with young people as well:

Covenant with the Missing Generation

It's the custom of the church to expect people to make commitments and promises as they come to be part of the church. This is a half-truth. In keeping with the God of grace who "first loved us," we must be the first to make promises to the missing generation as an act of grace, "first move love."

1. *We promise to meet you where you are*, literally and spiritually, and share the journey of mutual discovery to grow your own church for your generation in whatever place you feel at home. We repent of the arrogance that has imposed a uniformity that excluded you; and we renounce the arrogance that would exclude the catholicity of the wisdom of the ages for our journey together.

2. *We promise to listen and to keep on listening* beyond our settled frameworks of listening. We will listen to the rhythms of your life patterns and for your spirituality, explicit and implicit. We commit ourselves to respect the vulnerability of your unspoken pain and to offer opportunity for your unrealized potential.

3. *We promise to keep Jesus central* to all our explorations, for without him we have no identity. We repent of the secondary issues that have made it hard for you to meet him. We have

much to learn of the meaning of grace, and living the life-style of the Sermon on the Mount. We will travel together in small groups with Jesus at the center, mentoring each other on the way. We will discover ways of worshiping Father, Son, and Spirit that you and your generation will want to share.

4. *We promise you a community where you can belong and become if that is what you want.* We will remember the fun factor and make festival together. We will celebrate and respect the variety of temperaments and gifts you bring to worship and service. Structures will be simple, flexible, and functional, consistent with the life of Christ. There will be rhythms of stillness and activity. May *boredom* never be your word to describe our life together. (We cannot promise you that you will never be bored. That would be inhuman!)

5. *We promise the challenge of living life passionately for others* and the support of others as you work out the connections of living for God wherever you are. Bring your imagination, your creativity, and your passion, and let's see what God can create that's beyond our asking or imagining.

6. *We promise that we'll recognize Jesus Christ as the only leader of his church,* and we'll explore together how we help each other follow his lead. We renounce the misuse of any power and commit ourselves to the discipline of mutual listen-ing and mutual service. Leadership gifts will be recognized from within, not imposed from outside, but we'll always be accountable to the wider church in a spirit of humility and unity.

7. *We promise to live in the grace of our Lord Jesus Christ,* for we're all sinners and are bound to fail. We'll live by the spirit of mutual forgiveness and refuse to hold one another bondage to the dream of an ideal. We promise to love you as you are, as far as we are able, by the grace of God.

8. *We promise to keep asking the next question . . .*

OF BURNING
SHIPS AND
SINGING
NEW SONGS

As we invite our youth on the journey of faith, what picture is it that we frame for them in regard to what the grand community of God will look and feel like? As culture continues to shift and change around us, how will the church prepare youth for the world they will inherit?

The central thesis of this book has been a fairly basic one: Young people live in a complex, ever-shifting, ever-morphing world with multiple cultures and multiple resources by which they shape their sense of identity and their sense of faith. With the acceleration of technological connections and the tethered self becoming more and more a reality, the church needs to rethink not only how to approach these changes, but also what constitutes deep and vibrant faith in the twenty-first century. Part of the challenge is to remember that the goal of faith isn't merely having a right or wrong answer in some static survey or being able to completely articulate all the doctrines of the church by the time a young person graduates from high school. Faith is truly ever-changing, ever-growing, and ever-deepening.

Jesus constantly pointed to agricultural metaphors for the Christian life: the amazing growth of a mustard plant, the beauty of lilies in the fields, the wheat harvest, and scattered seeds across many soils, to name just a few. What's important to note in all of these metaphors for faith is that growth occurs as much under the earth as it does above the ground. True, bearing fruit and stretching ever higher for the light of the sun is vital. But so, too, are the roots that seek out living water and nutrients for that fruit to grow into fullness.

To understand young people as blurring the boundaries of identity and culture in order to move between and betwixt areas of meaning is to acknowledge that there's a lot going on beneath the surface that we just don't experience—but nevertheless there's growth at work. As I started this book with the tale of William 1.0 and 2.0, I come back to the story of these young men as not yet completed. Roots that have been growing for years are only now starting to offer up fruit above ground. The myriad ways in which they've both made sense of their lives are coming together in ways I never would have predicted, but in God's economy something beautiful is happening.

In order for us to embrace the challenge of working with this generation of young people, we have to be willing to radically embrace the wonder of these blurred identities who are constantly in motion, checking in and checking out of our programs, reading YA novels that might seem counter to our sensibilities, listening to music that might not mention Jesus by name, watching videos that call for a level of transcendence and mystery that might take us to new conversations. This will mean a commitment to the process of being with this generation right where they are—not necessarily where we as leaders in the church have found safe harbor.

In 1519, Hernán Cortés, the Castilian conquistador whose expedition to the Americas would eventually result in the fall of the Aztec Empire, landed on the shore and committed himself to this new land with a move more radical than most missionaries would ever make: he set fire to the ships that carried him from Spain. Evoking Cortés may certainly seem antithetical to the cause of the gospel, but the radical action of his abandonment is not. In many respects, this is a Christlike turn as exhibited by Jesus taking the form of a servant in Philippians 2 and "emptying himself" for the sake of those he loves. As adults who work with youth, we have a call to set fire to the ships and make our home in a place where young people are making sense of faith in seemingly strange ways. In some respects we must commit to abandon the hope of returning to some golden era of the church as something apart and separate from culture.

For some of us in youth ministry, this call will mean setting fire to the need for our students to see having their own youth ministry (one church = one youth ministry) as "something every church does" and choose the Christlike move toward binding the youth ministry of their church to another church for the sake of community. For others, this call will mean setting fire to the places of isolation from culture and moving more fully to the places of hospitality by closing some of our churches altogether and merging and binding our lives to others, rather than opening more arenas of separation. For some it will mean choosing to forgo the pulpit or the programmatic youth position with a safe salary in order to model sitting under another person's leadership and sacrificing ourselves for the sake of the kingdom of God. Or it could mean setting fire to that need to grow in numbers if it means uniformity as the fast track, which is a challenge in hard economic realities.

In short, this "releasing call" that the Christlike turn provokes for us is ultimately more than laying down some aspect of who we are—it's often setting fire to all that we have been, embracing the risk of becoming something altogether new beyond the event horizon. It's a call to empty ourselves and to empty our proverbial backpacks of privileges for the sake of the journey of reconciliation with the young people in the culture around us, even if we didn't consciously put the privileges there. It's a call to realize the load we carry might be light for us but a heavy burden for those around us.

The song that plays during Disneyland's "It's a Small World" ride has it right: "It's a world of laughter, / A world of tears. / It's a world of hopes, / And a world of fears. / There's so much that we share, / That it's time we're aware, / It's a small world after all." Rather than ride the boat while passively listening to the song, perhaps it's time to step onto land and set fire to the ship that brought us to this place, committing ourselves to staying, living, and loving more deeply than we could have if we'd maintained an escape boat parked on the shoreline.

Perhaps by committing ourselves to this task we can also learn to sing a new song, not one written by the culture *per se*, but the *Carmen Christi* or "hymn of Christ" found in Philippians 2. Paul offers us a form and depth of life that is infinitely more profound as we are challenged by the call of Christ's life to choose the "form" of faith as cohabitation with others. We are called to "get personal" within the lives of each other as reconciliation for the sake of the gospel. And this is to happen in the midst of the cultures as we walk alongside young people who will be the future of the church.

ACKNOWLEDGMENTS

The writing of this book ended on an interesting anniversary of sorts in popular culture. In 1965, Bob Dylan was at the peak of his early career in music when he performed at the Newport Folk Festival. Much to the shock of the audience and music critics gathered on the evening of July 25, 1965, Dylan stepped out for his set and performed not as an acoustic artist, but with a full band that was literally and figuratively electric. Famously the event elicited boos from the audience and even jeers. Many called Dylan a "Judas" for betraying the implicit mandate that a folk artist adhere to the forms that had been handed down to him by Woody Guthrie and others.

Stepping onstage at that time in music as a very real standard-bearer in folk music and risking new ways of considering what is orthodox takes prophetic courage and a pretty thick skin. Sitting on this side of history allows us to view a moment like this from a comfortable place. Dylan not only survived the concert and being called a Judas, but he also ultimately redefined his sound as well as the sound of generations multiple times since then. He's an example of an artist who was willing to see the movement and change of form not as an enemy to fight, but often a prophetic voice to heed.

While I'm in no way aligning myself with the genius of Bob Dylan, I do believe youth ministry is at a decidedly interesting crossroads where the tried-and-true forms that have been implicitly accepted in how we engage teenagers, the role of the church is in the midst of popular culture, and the boundaries and categories by which we situated our point of view on teens is shaking and becoming increasingly blurred—hence the title and themes of the book. Should the Lord lead, there's a need to step onto the stage every once and a while and "go electric." I'm not sure if this book and its thesis regarding sacredly mobile adolescents is that moment, but I constantly pray for moments like that one at the Newport Folk Festival to fall upon the church and youth ministry.

I come to youth ministry and my work as a professor, past youth leader, and father of middle schoolers with humility borne after years of teens correcting my assumptions; many friends, parents, and colleagues challenging and compassionately correcting me; and the gracious, constant movement of the Holy Spirit quieting my fears and lifting my chin to look no longer at the past, but to where the Lord is leading me even as I stumble and fall.

I'm so thankful to many people who shaped and encouraged this project along the way, especially the editing work of Heather Campbell, Ginny Olson, and members of the Zondervan team who believed in this project from beginning to end. Andrew David played a vital role in reading and editing an early draft of this book—his recommendations were invaluable. My colleagues at Seattle Pacific University in the School of Theology; the many volunteers in Young Life and Youth for Christ that I've had as students, friends, and coworkers; Youth Specialties and the faith and conviction of my brothers and sisters in Christ who have prayed through the various seasons of this project.

Parts of this book have been rewritten from previous research projects, and I'm grateful for the permission to draw from those sources to create the chapters found in this text: chapter 3 was originally offered as the 2013 Weter Lecture at

Seattle Pacific University, and I'm grateful to the Faculty Status Committee and Center for Scholarship & Faculty Development for the space and time to develop these reflections on Walter Brueggemann in relation to the work of the National Study for Youth and Religion.

Chapter 5 was drawn from a study conducted with a former student and published as "The Sacredly Mobile Adolescent—A Hermeneutic Phenomenological Study Toward Revising of the Third Culture Kid Typology for Effective Ministry Practice in a Multivalent Culture" in *Journal of Youth Ministry*, Fall 2009.

Chapter 6 was originally a longer discussion of the contributions of St. Augustine to understandings of popular culture titled "Confessions on the Dance Floor: St. Augustine and the Sacred Mobility of Subjectivity in Youth Culture" in *Journal of Youth and Theology*, Volume 8, Number 2, November 2009.

Chapter 7 draws part of its reflections on C. S. Lewis from the article "The Beatific Quest as Faith Formation in C. S. Lewis's The Chronicles of Narnia: Direction, Release and Integration" published in *The Other Journal: Journal of Theology and Culture*, #15—Aesthetics Issue, July 14, 2009.

My reflections on the heritage of the *Bildungsroman* and coming-of-age found in chapter 8 were drawn from a longer reflection on the German writer Johannes Goethe titled "Seeing and Being with Youth: *Bildungsroman* and Coming of Age from Goethe to Star Wars and The Matrix" first published in *Journal of Youth and Theology*, Volume 2, Number 5, November 2006. I am thankful to the publishers of these journals for allowing my work to be revised for this project.

Lastly, I dedicate this book to my three daughters Clara, Eilidh, and Miriam. Over the years they've proven to be three of the most wise, insightful, and joyful readers of life and culture anyone could have. They're proof to me every day of God's grandeur and delight, as well as the sacred mobility of human development as they continue to spin, jump, turn, fall down laughing, and rise again to dance and sing in harmony with the Spirit of the Lord who's neither still nor silent. As in Ezekiel's vision in chapter 37, they continue to teach these old bones to dance.

BIBLIOGRAPHY

Ammerman, N. T. *Congregation and Community*. New Brunswick, NJ: Rutgers University Press, 1997.

Ammerman, N. T., ed. *Everyday Religion: Observing Modern Religious Lives*. New York: Oxford University Press, 2007.

Appadurai, A. *Modernity at Large: Cultural Dimensions of Globalization*. Minneapolis and London: University of Minnesota Press, 1996.

Augustine. *De vera religione* [Of True Religion] In J. H. S. Burleigh (Trans.), *Augustine: Early Writings*. London: SCM Press, 1953. (Original work written in AD 390.)

Austin, C. N., and J. Beyer. "Missionary Repatriation: An Introduction to the Literature." *International Bulletin of Missionary Research 8*(2) (1984), 68–71.

Balthasar, H. U. von. *Engagement with God: The Drama of Christian Discipleship*. San Francisco: Ignatius Press, 2008.

Bantum, B. "Why Christians Can't Be Post-Racial: Christian Existence in the Murky Waters of Race and Place." *The Other Journal: Journal of Theology and Culture 16* (2009). Retrieved from http://theotherjournal.com/article.php?id=851.

Barth, K. *Church Dogmatics IV.3.1: The Doctrine of Reconciliation*. 1st ed. New York: T&T Clark International, 2004.

Beaudoin, T. *Witness to Dispossession*. New York: Orbis, 2008.

Bergler, T. *The Juvenilization of American Christianity*. Grand Rapids, MI: Eerdmans, 2012.

Bonhoeffer, D. *The Communion of Saints (Sanctorum Communio)*. New York: Harper & Row, 1963.

Bonhoeffer, D. *Ethics*. New York: Macmillan Publishing, 1955.

Bonhoeffer, D. *Letters and Papers from Prison*. Updated Version. New York: Touchstone, 1997.

Bonhoeffer, D. *Life Together*. New York: HarperCollins, 1954.

Bourdieu, P. *Distinction: A Social Critique of the Judgment of Taste*. Translated by Richard Nice. Cambridge, MA: Harvard University Press, 1984.

Bradley, I. *Colonies of Heaven: Celtic Models for Today's Church*. London: Dartman, Longman & Todd, 2000.

Carter, J. K. *Race: A Theological Account*. Oxford, U.K.: Oxford University Press, 2008.

Clark, C. *Hurt: Inside the World of Today's Teenagers*. Grand Rapids, MI: Baker Academic, 2004.

Cronin, K. *Kenosis: Emptying Self and the Path of Christian Service*. London: Continuum, 2005.

Dean, K., ed. *Starting Right: Thinking Theologically about Youth Ministry*. Grand Rapids, MI: Zondervan, 2001.

Derrida, J. *The Gift of Death*. Translated by David Wills. Chicago: University of Chicago Press, 1996.

Derrida, J. *Monolingualism of the Other: or, The Prosthesis of Origin*. Translated by Patrick Mensah. Mieke Bal and Hent de Vries, series eds. Cultural Memory in the Present. Stanford, CA: Stanford University Press, 1991.

Dougherty, K. D. "How Monochromatic Is Church

Membership?: Racial-Ethnic Diversity in Religious Community." *Sociology of Religion* 64(1) (2003), 65–85.

Edwards, M. J., and T. C. Oden, eds. *Ancient Christian Commentary on Scripture: New Testament Vol. 8. Galatians, Ephesians, Philippians.* Downers Grove, IL: InterVarsity Press, 1999.

Elkind, D. *All Grown Up and No Place to Go: Teenagers in Crisis.* Reading, PA: Addison-Wesley, 1984.

Emerson, M. O., and C. Smith. *Divided by Faith: Evangelical Religion and the Problem of Race in America.* Oxford, U.K.: Oxford University Press, 2000.

Evans, C. S. *Exploring Kenotic Christology: The Self-Emptying of God.* Oxford, U.K.: Oxford University Press, 2006.

Fee, G. D. "The New Testament and Kenosis Christology." In C. S. Evans ed., *Exploring Kenotic Christology: The Self-Emptying of God.* (pp. 25–44). New York: Oxford University Press, 2006.

Garber, S. *The Fabric of Faithfulness: Weaving Together Belief and Behavior.* Expanded ed. Downers Grove, IL: InterVarsity Press, 2007.

Glaser, B. B., and A. L. Strauss. *The Discovery of Grounded Theory.* Chicago: Adline de Gruyter, 1967.

Gorman, M. J. *Inhabiting the Cruciform God: Kenosis, Justification, and Theosis in Paul's Narrative Soteriology.* Grand Rapids, MI: Eerdmans, 2009.

Hall, G. S. *Adolescence: Its Psychology and Its Relations to Physiology, Anthropology, Sociology, Crime, Religion and Education.* (Vol. 2). New York: Appleton, 1904.

Hopkins, D. *Being Human: Race, Culture and Religion.* Minneapolis: Fortress Press, 2005.

Huntington, S. *The Clash of Civilizations and the Remaking of World Order.* New York: Simon and Schuster, 1998.

Kett, Joseph. *Rites of Passage: Adolescence in America 1790 to the Present.* (New York, Basic Books, 1977) 3-4..

Keuss, J. "Seeing and Being with Youth: *Bildungsroman* and Coming of Age from Goethe to Star Wars and The Matrix." *Journal of Youth and Theology* 2(5) (November 2006), 29–48.

Keuss, J. F., and R. Willett. "The Sacredly Mobile Adolescent: A Hermeneutic Phenomenological Study Toward Revising of the Third Culture Kid Typology for Effective Ministry Practice in a Multivalent Culture." *Journal of Youth Ministry* 8(1) (Fall 2009), 7–24.

Lévi-Strauss, C. *The Savage Mind.* Translated by Julian Pitt-Rivers. Chicago: University of Chicago Press, 1966.

McIntosh, P. "White Privilege: Unpacking the Invisible Knapsack." *Peace and Freedom.* (July/August 1989).

Nouwen, H. J. M. *Creative Ministry.* Revised Image Books ed. New York: Random House, 2003.

Nouwen, H. J. M. *Life of the Beloved.* New York: Crossroad, 1992.

O'Connell Killen, P., and M. Silk. eds. *Religion and Public Life in the Pacific Northwest: The None Zone.* Religion by Region Series. Lanham, MD: AltaMira Press, 2004.

Pearce, L., and M. Denton. *A Faith of Their Own: Stability and Change in the Religiosity of America's Adolescents.* New York: Oxford University Press, 2011.

Pollock, D. C., and R. E. Van Reken. *Third Culture Kids.* New York: Nicholas Brealey Publishing, 1999.

Root, A. *Revisiting Relational Youth Ministry: From a Strategy of Influence to a Theology of Incarnation.* Downers Grove, IL: InterVarsity Press, 2007.

Sanders, C. *Ministry at the Margins: The Prophetic Mission of Women, Youth and the Poor.* Downers Grove, IL: InterVarsity Press, 1997.

Schumacher, E. F. *Small Is Beautiful: Economics as if People Mattered.* San Francisco: Harper Perennial, 1989.

Smith, C., et. al. *Lost in Transition: The Dark Side of Emerging Adulthood.* New York: Oxford University Press, 2011.

Smith, C., and M. L. Denton. *Soul Searching: The Religious and Spiritual Lives of American Teenagers.* New York: Oxford University Press, 2009.

Smith, J. K. A. *Desiring the Kingdom: Worship, Worldview, and Cultural Formation.* Grand Rapids, MI: Baker Books, 2009.

Swinton, J., and H. Mowat. *Practical Theology and Qualitative Research.* London: SCM, 2006.

Tatum, B. D. *Why Are All the Black Kids Sitting Together in the Cafeteria? A Psychologist Explains the Development of Racial Identity.* 5th rev. ed. New York: Basic Books, 2003.

Taylor, C. *Sources of the Self.* Cambridge, MA: Harvard University Press, 1989.

Turkle, S. *Life on the Screen: Identity in the Age of the Internet.* New York: Simon & Schuster, 1997.

Unseem, R. H. "Education of Third Culture Children: An Annotated Bibliography." *Studies in Third Cultures: A Continuing Series* (No. 1). East Lansing, MI: Institute for International Studies in Education, 1971.

Van Manen, M. *Researching Lived Experience: Human Science*

for an Action Sensitive Pedagogy. New York: State University of New York Press, 1990.

Wagner, C. P. *Our Kind of People: The Ethical Dimensions of Church Growth in America.* Atlanta: John Knox Press, 1979.

Wellmen, J. *Evangelical vs. Liberal.* New York: Oxford University Press, 2007.

Wenger, D. F. "Three Generations of Third Culture Kids." *Brethren in Christ History and Life. 29*(3) (2006), 256.

White, D. F. "The Vocation of Youth . . . as Youth." *Insights: The Faculty Journal of Austin Seminary, 123*(2) (2008), 3–12.

Wuthnow, R. J. "Taking Talk Seriously: Religious Discourse as Social Practice," *Journal for the Scientific Study of Religion 50*(1) (March 1, 2011).

Share Your Thoughts

With the Author: Your comments will be forwarded to the author when you send them to *zauthor@zondervan.com*.

With Zondervan: Submit your review of this book by writing to *zreview@zondervan.com*.

Free Online Resources at
www.zondervan.com

Daily Bible Verses and Devotions: Enrich your life with daily Bible verses or devotions that help you start every morning focused on God. Visit www.zondervan.com/newsletters.

Free Email Publications: Sign up for newsletters on Christian living, academic resources, church ministry, fiction, children's resources, and more. Visit www.zondervan.com/newsletters.

Zondervan Bible Search: Find and compare Bible passages in a variety of translations at www.zondervanbiblesearch.com.

Other Benefits: Register to receive online benefits like coupons and special offers, or to participate in research.